T0293913

WALKING THE BRITTANY COAST PATH

THE GR34 FROM MONT-SAINT-MICHEL TO ROSCOFF

by Carroll Dorgan

JUNIPER HOUSE, MURLEY MOSS,
OXENHOLME ROAD, KENDAL, CUMBRIA LA9 7RL
www.cicerone.co.uk

Printed in Czechia on responsibly sourced paper on behalf of Latitude Press Limited
A catalogue record for this book is available from the British Library.
All photographs are by the author unless otherwise stated.

Route mapping by Lovell Johns www.lovelljohns.com
Contains OpenStreetMap.org data © OpenStreetMap contributors, CC-BY-SA. NASA relief data courtesy of ESRI

The routes of the GR®, PR® and GRP® paths in this guide have been reproduced with the permission of the Fédération Française de la Randonnée Pédestre holder of the exclusive rights of the routes. The names GR®, PR® and GRP® are registered trademarks. © FFRP 2022 for all GR®, PR® and GRP® paths appearing in this work.

To Emily and Chloé, who follow in my footsteps – and blaze new trails.

Note on mapping

The route maps in this guide are derived from publicly available data, databases and crowd-sourced data. As such they have not been through the detailed checking procedures that would generally be applied to a published map from an official mapping agency. However, we have reviewed them closely in the light of local knowledge as part of the preparation of this guide.

Front cover: Ploumanac'h lighthouse (Stage 20)

CONTENTS

On the Pink Granite Coast (Stage 20)

ROUTE SUMMARY TABLE

Stage	Start	Distance	Ascent	Descent	Time	Page
1	Mont-Saint-Michel	19.5km	185m	175m	5hr	36
2	Saint-Broladre	30.5km	310m	320m	7hr 30min	41
3	Cancale	22km	860m	845m	5hr 45min	48
4	La Guimorais	12.5km	180m	195m	3hr 30min	52
5	Saint-Malo	20km/33.5km	485m/825m	470m/795m	5hr/8hr 30min	58
6	Lancieux	32.5km	690m	710m	8hr	64
7	Saint-Cast-le-Guildo	17.5km	585m	485m	4hr 30min	70
8	Petit Trécelin	22km	825m	875m	6hr	75
9	Sables-d'Or-les-Pins	21km	660m	655m	5hr 15min	80
10	Pléneuf-Val-André	26.5km	930m	930m	6hr 45min	86
11	Hillion	17km	275m	230m	4hr	91
12	Saint-Laurent-de-la-Mer	26km	980m	1005m	7hr	97
13	Saint-Quay-Portrieux	20km	940m	935m	5hr 15min	103
14	Bréhec	21km	625m	635m	5hr 45min	108
15	Paimpol	25km	655m	635m	5hr 45min	113
16	Lézardrieux	19km	315m	335m	5hr	119
17	Le Québo	20km	365m	360m	5hr 45min	125

Stage	Start	Distance	Ascent	Descent	Time	Page
18	Tréguier	29.5km	525m	525m	8hr 15min	129
19	Port Blanc	15km	255m	250m	3hr 45min	134
20	Perros-Guirec	17.5km	330m	325m	4hr	138
21	Trégastel (Coz Pors)	15.5km/22.5km	190m/255m	195m/260m	4hr/5hr 45min	143
22	Île Grande	30.5km	850m	810m	9hr	148
23	Le Yaudet	27km	825m	860m	8hr	154
24	Locquirec	20km (variant 18.5km)	910m (variant 490m)	840m (variant 440m)	6hr (variant 5hr 15min)	159
25	Plougasnou	13.5km	300m	370m	3hr 45min	164
26	Saint-Samson	21km	365m	365m	5hr	167
27	Morlaix	22.5km	605m	570m	5hr 45min	173
28	Carantec	20km	290m	315m	5hr	182
	Total	624km	approx. 15,700m	approx. 15,700m	28 days	

The coast on the western side of the Baie de l'Arguenon (Stage 6)

INTRODUCTION

The distance between Mont-Saint-Michel and Roscoff is 170km as the herring gull flies. If you walk along the GR34 trail from Mont-Saint-Michel to Roscoff, it's 624km – and you'll see a lot more of Brittany than that gull!

The GR34 is a coastal path, and the north Brittany coast is highly indented. This is the 'Sentier des Douaniers' (Customs Officers' Path). In the perpetual game of cat-and-mouse between customs officers and smugglers, no section of the coast could be ignored. Hence, the path traces virtually every cove, estuary, bay and headland of the coast. The Sentier des Douaniers was established in 1791 (incorporating earlier infrastructure)

but had fallen into disuse by the 20th century. Smugglers had not given up the game, of course; they simply used different techniques and routes – often with different contraband. In 1968, work began to restore the Sentier des Douaniers as a recreational hiking route, designated GR34 (Grande Randonnée 34). Today, the GR34 is one of the leading long-distance hiking paths in France. Its length around the coast, from Mont-Saint-Michel to Saint-Nazaire, exceeds 2000km.

In 2018, the GR34 between Locquirec and Saint-Pol-de-Léon was voted the favourite GR of the French in a poll organised by the national hiking association (FFRandonnée).

A discreet cove (Saint-Quiriou) between Le Yaudet and Locquémeau (Stage 23)

You will walk along that section of the GR34 during the last five stages covered by this guidebook, and you may well agree with the vote. Or you may have a different favourite: perhaps the Emerald Coast (Côte d'Émeraude) between Cancale and Cap Fréhel (Stages 3–8) or the Pink Granite Coast (Côte de Granit Rose) between Perros-Guirec and Trébeurden (Stages 20–22). Or what about the cliffs and beaches between Saint-Laurent-de-la-Mer and Paimpol (Stages 12–14)? It's hard to choose!

If you have limited time, you might choose to walk a short section of the GR34. Appendix A suggests four 5-day itineraries based on some of the route's highlights – two sections of the Emerald Coast (Pointe du Grouin and Cap Fréhel), the Pink Granite Coast and Morlaix Bay – with stage breakdowns and notes on getting to and from the trail.

WHAT IT'S LIKE TO HIKE ON THE NORTH BRITTANY COAST

One outstanding feature of hiking along the GR34 is variety. There are memorable traverses across steep slopes high above rocky shores where waves crash, such as between Pointe du Grouin and Pointe du Meinga (Stage 3) and from Locquémeau to Saint-Michel-en-Grève (Stage 23). Elsewhere, the trail stays closer to the water, passing innumerable beaches. Some of those beaches are vast expanses of sand in front of towns that attract many visitors; others are cosy crescents of sand, barely accessible to anyone but a walker on the GR34. The trail also passes through forests and crosses heathland, often beside coastal cliffs and in sight of the sea. The heathland sparkles in the spring with yellow gorse and broom, complemented in the summer by purple heather.

The GR34 is not a mountain trail; there are extensive sections of level walking. The trail does, however, climb and descend many slopes – never for very long, but steep in places. You'll climb more than 900m during Stage 24 (and descend an equivalent amount), with fantastic views of the sea rewarding your efforts. In short, a trek on the GR34 is relatively easy but occasionally strenuous.

As you would expect, tides sometimes govern this coastal trail. There are short sections of the GR34 that may be submerged at high tide. Variants, mentioned in the text and broadly indicated on the maps of this book, can be followed when high tide blocks the main route. These high-tide variants are easy to follow, as they are clearly marked, with signs at the two ends of the variant trail (for example: 'VARIANTE PAR MARÉE HAUTE') and GR marks. IGN maps (see 'Maps', below) show the variants, along with the GR34 itself. Tide tables are posted on tourist office websites and can be purchased at tobacconists (*tabacs*). Most convenient are smartphone apps that provide detailed information about tides at numerous places along the coast (for example, http://maree.info).

You may also encounter detours resulting from rockfalls or mudslides (*éboulements*) along this coastal trail: a barrier blocks the trail with an explanatory sign and occasionally a map showing the alternate route. You will observe that the GR34 is maintained: you may meet teams of workers cutting back grass and bushes that encroach upon the trail. Give them a smile and wave of thanks!

Urban life may seem remote as you lean into the wind while walking around a rocky headland, but there will be a warm bed at the end of the stage – or a sleeping bag, if you choose to camp. Large towns – Saint-Malo, Dinard, Saint-Brieuc, Paimpol, Lannion, Morlaix – offer accommodation, restaurants and public transport (including railway service), not to mention historic buildings, museums and other interesting attractions. You will be welcomed with warm hospitality in small towns such as Cancale, Erquy, Tréguier, Perros-Guirec, Ploumanac'h, Trébeurden and Roscoff. If you spend the night in a village where there is no restaurant, your host may provide a meal (*table d'hôte*) or drive you to a nearby restaurant for dinner and return to pick you up at the end of the meal.

GEOLOGY

The story of Brittany's geology is a long one – indeed, longer than most. It starts with the oldest rocks in France: a band of exposed Icartian basement

Trail maintenance on Stage 11

extending from Trébeurden past Ploumanac'h and across Guernsey's Icart Point to the Cotentin Peninsula. There isn't space here to describe all that happened on the Armorican Massif after this metamorphic gneiss was formed 2 billion years ago – but there are geological features of the north Brittany coast that will certainly interest a trekker on the GR34.

For example, the pink sandstone cliffs around Cap Fréhel, standing 70m above the sea, are an awesome sight. These cliffs were formed from sand and clay deposited around 460 million years ago (late Cambrian/early Ordovician). The horizontal strata of this sedimentary rock stand out; iron oxides give the rock its pink tint.

The pink granite boulders between Perros-Guirec and Trébeurden will dazzle and astonish you. How were they formed? How did they get there? Another long story: around 300 million years ago, during the Hercynian orogeny (mountain formation), magma rose from below the earth's crust and filled spaces in the basement rock. The magma cooled and crystallised very slowly, forming granite composed of quartz, mica and feldspar. (The feldspar gives this granite its pink tint.) The slow crystallisation of the granite left minute cracks in the rock. Water penetrated these cracks and caused erosion that produced rounded forms of granite rock surrounded by coarse granitic sand. Eventually, the Hercynian mountains were mostly eroded away, leaving granite boulders exposed on the surface – and subject to further erosion by water, wind and fluctuations of temperature.

Granite boulders at Le Castel (Trébeurden, Stage 22)

A ria (Jaudy River near Tréguier) on Stage 17

The post-glacial rise of sea levels during the Quaternary period partially submerged unglaciated river valleys, creating long tidal estuaries called rias that contribute to the highly indented form of the coast. There are no bridges across the outlets of the rias in our section of the GR34 (although a 'sea bus' links Saint-Malo and Dinard across the Rance estuary). Therefore, you will walk inland on one side of a ria, cross a bridge (for example at Lannion) and then walk back out the opposite side.

WILDLIFE

The rocky headlands and islands along the Breton coast are the home – or at least the nesting place – for many seabirds. One of the best places to observe these birds is Cap Fréhel, a bird sanctuary. A big, guano-covered rock, Fauconnière, stands just offshore. You may see European shag and several species of gulls. Some pelagic birds (those that live far offshore and return to land only to breed) come to Cap Fréhel each spring: northern fulmar, Manx shearwater and common murre.

In the 19th century, more than 15,000 couples of Atlantic puffins made their nests each year along this coast. Rapacious hunting of these 'clowns of the sea' threatened to wipe out the species in this area. In 1912, the League for the Protection of Birds (Ligue pour la Protection des Oiseaux, LPO) was established and a sanctuary was created specifically to save the puffins: the Réserve des Sept-Îles. About 200 puffin couples now breed there. Other birds flock to the Sept-Îles, in particular the northern gannet, Europe's largest seabird. The gannet catches its prey (mackerel, sardines, sprat) by plunging vertically into the sea at speeds up to 100km/h – a spectacular sight. Excursions by boat to observe the islands and their birds depart from Perros-Guirec.

The vast Saint-Brieuc Bay teems with migratory birds during the winter; some pause here during their travels, while others spend the entire winter around the bay. The sandworms and other invertebrates in the mud and small fish and shellfish in the water attract wading birds such as oystercatchers, grey herons and sandpipers. There are also mallards, common shelducks and brant geese.

The wildlife of this area includes many mammals, of course, but you may, at best, get only a fleeting glimpse of them as you walk through their habitat: deer, rabbits and hares, foxes, otters and badgers. There are also aquatic mammals: grey seals live around the Réserve des Sept-Îles, and you might see dolphins cavorting along the Emerald Coast.

HISTORY

Prehistoric times

Human settlement in Brittany dates back some 700,000 years, but we can skip forward to the fifth–third millennia BCE, when the great megaliths were built. Of course, there are megaliths in many areas of Europe (Stonehenge comes to mind), but these stone tombs and monuments are particularly associated with Brittany – rightly so, according to recent research: Dr Bettina Schulz Paulsson, in a paper published in 2019, concluded that 'the earliest megaliths originated in northwest France and spread along the sea routes of the Mediterranean and Atlantic coasts'.

Brittany's megaliths include menhirs (standing stones) and gallery graves, such as dolmen and *allées couvertes* (large flat stones placed upon upright ones). Several small megaliths stand near the GR34 (as noted in the text). And then there is the Cairn de Barnénez – the largest megalith in Europe (Stage 26). Don't miss it!

The Bronze Age (2400–600 BCE) brought development and prosperity, as Brittany was a source of the tin used to make bronze. During the later Iron Age (450–50 BCE), the Celtic culture that spread across Europe reached Brittany. The Celtic name for the area was Armorica ('the land facing the sea'); it was part of what the Romans called Gaul.

Armorica

As Rome extended its power into Gaul, Armoricans resisted interference with their profitable trade with Britain. Rome's ambitious governor of Gaul, Julius Caesar, sent his legions into Armorica. His fleet's defeat of the Veneti, redoubtable seafarers, in Quiberon Bay (56 BCE) was the decisive event in Rome's conquest of Armorica.

ASTÉRIX AND THE CHARIOT RACE

In *Astérix et la Transitalique* (2017), the 'Lupus' (wolf) brand of garum sponsored a chariot race from Modicia (Monza) to Neapolis (Naples) with the slogan: 'Garum Lupus, le condiment des champions'. To win the race, Astérix and Obélix had to defeat a wily Roman named... Coronavirus.

Armorica became part of the Lugdunensis province. Roman roads helped to integrate Armorica in the flourishing economic life of the High Empire. Romanised *élites* built villas and enjoyed the pleasures of thermal baths. The GR34 passes the ruins of the Hogolo baths near Plestin-les-Grèves (Stage 23).

Armorica produced and exported garum, a strongly flavoured sauce made with fermented fish intestines and salt that was very popular in the Roman world. Some varieties were considered delicacies (*garum sociorum*, made with mackerel and lauded by Pliny the Elder, was the best), while Armorica's lower-grade garum was destined for the army. Roman legionaries stationed beside Hadrian's Wall probably seasoned their rations with Armorican garum.

Political instability, inflation and military disasters wreaked havoc in the Roman Empire during the third century. Armorica was not spared, as Saxon pirates raided its coasts. The reigns of Diocletian (284–305) and

Ruins of the Roman Hogolo thermal baths (Stage 23)

his immediate successors brought ephemeral relief. Strong points on the Armorican coast were fortified, including places on the GR34: Alet (near Saint-Malo) and Le Yaudet. Many of the soldiers manning these forts came from Britain – precursors of the migrations that would transform Armorica.

Instability returned in the fourth century, leading eventually to the collapse of the Roman Empire in the West in the fifth century. During this time and continuing into the seventh century, many Britons migrated to Armorica, under pressure from Anglo-Saxon invaders. Religious leaders, including seven remembered as 'Founder Saints', guided the Britons in Armorica. The Britons brought their version of Christianity and their Celtic language, which evolved into Breton: Armorica became Brittany.

In the centuries after the fall of the Western Roman Empire, Brittany comprised several petty tribal kingdoms. The rise of the Carolingian Franks brought a strong, aggressive power to the Breton borderlands. Breton leaders resisted attacks by Charlemagne and his successors. They consolidated their power and gained recognition as kings of Brittany, in return for pledges of fealty to the Carolingians. However, a Breton king, Erispoë, was assassinated in 857 by his cousin, Salomon, who, in turn, was murdered by members of his family. The kingdom did not survive the ensuing civil strife and devastating Viking attacks. It was

only in 937, when Alain Barbe-Torte – a Breton nobleman – returned to Brittany from exile, that stable, strong rule was restored. Alain drove the Vikings out of Brittany and took the title of duke. The Duchy of Brittany was born.

Duchy of Brittany

A theme that runs through the six centuries of the Duchy's existence is its struggle to maintain (or recover) independence. Bretons faced pressure and outright attacks from France and England. Resisting one often entailed seeking assistance from the other.

The death of Duke Arthur produced a moment of drama: Arthur (1187–1203), the son of Geoffrey (son of Henry II, King of England) and Constance (daughter of Conan IV, Duke of Brittany), had claims to rule both England and Brittany. Arthur disappeared under suspicious circumstances after being captured by his uncle, King John of England. It is believed that John ordered the killing of Arthur (or even did the deed himself). In Shakespeare's *King John*, Arthur leaps to his death from a castle wall, uttering his final words: 'Heaven take my soul, and England keep my bones!'

The death in 1341 of Duke Jean III without a legitimate child or designated successor led to the War of Succession, which lasted more than 20 years and was drawn into the Anglo-French Hundred Years War. The most famous battle was the 'Combat des Trente': a group of 30 Anglo-Bretons fought 30 Franco-Bretons at a time and place agreed in advance. Froissart and other medieval chroniclers celebrated this spectacle of chivalry, but to the modern eye it appears more suited to a Monty Python sketch.

The Duchy reached its apogee in the 15th century. The Breton Estates – an assembly comprising members of the three orders of society (clergy, nobility and commoners) – convened with broader representation and approved direct taxes to finance the duchy's ever-growing needs, ranging from its army to the dukes' lavish lifestyles. A university was established in Nantes (1460). Maritime commerce grew in importance, and production of textiles increased.

However, as France recovered from war and weak leadership, its kings turned their attention to nominal vassals who defied their authority. The French invaded Brittany and defeated a Breton army in 1488. Duke François II agreed that his daughters would not marry without the French king's consent – and died a few weeks later. His daughter Anne succeeded him as Duchess of Brittany. She was 11 years old.

Anne married the French king, Charles VIII, in 1491. After Charles' accidental death (he bumped his head on a lintel in the Amboise château), Anne married his successor, Louis XII, in 1499. The couple's daughter, Claude, brought the Duchy of Brittany as her dowry when she married François d'Angoulême shortly after Anne's death in 1514. Angoulême acceded to the French throne as François I.

Province of the Ancien Régime

François completed the process of extinguishing Brittany's independence

A **corps de garde** (*customs officer's watch house, Stage 3*)

in 1532: wielding both carrots and sticks, he induced the Breton Estates to request union with France. François issued edicts that implemented the perpetual union of Brittany with the Kingdom of France, while stipulating that Brittany's traditional rights, liberties and privileges would be maintained. Among those privileges was one that will interest a trekker on the Sentier des Douaniers: Brittany remained exempt from the *gabelle* (salt tax) – a tax that was onerous elsewhere. Differences in the price of salt – for example, 56–58 *livres* per quintal (100kg) in neighbouring Maine and Anjou, compared to 2–3 *livres* in Brittany – created irresistible incentives for smuggling. Jacques Necker, Louis XVI's finance minister, reported in 1784 that more than 23,000 men were deployed to stop the smuggling of salt and other commodities. Some of those men were stationed in the watch houses (*corps de garde*) that you will pass on the Sentier des Douaniers.

Brittany initially prospered as a province of France. Cereal production and stock raising flourished. Flax and hemp were grown to produce excellent linen and canvas. Indeed, England imported canvas for the Royal Navy's sailcloth from Brittany because its quality was superior to cloth produced at home. Breton sailors fished for cod in the bountiful waters around Newfoundland and found ready markets for their catch in the Catholic lands of the Mediterranean. Breton towns vied to display their wealth and piety by building magnificent *enclos paroissiaux* (parish closes), one of which can be visited in Saint-Jean-du-Doigt near the GR34 (Stage 24). However, there was a stain upon this prosperity: from the late 17th century, Breton ports – in particular, Nantes – played a leading role in the profitable transatlantic slave trade.

Brittany's prosperity and stability were shaken in the century after 1675. Wars disrupted Brittany's maritime commerce, as did mercantilist policies

A seagull on Saint-Malo's ramparts, with Fort National in the background (Stage 4)

implemented by Louis XIV's finance minister, Jean-Baptiste Colbert. The imposition of new taxes without the consent of the Breton Estates provoked recurrent crises. For example, protests against new taxes to finance a war against the Netherlands erupted in towns in 1675. Unrest soon spread to the countryside, where peasants (known for the caps they wore as the *bonnets rouges*) attacked nobles and articulated demands for radical social reforms. The governor of the province, the Duc de Chaulnes, sent in troops who brutally suppressed the protests. So many were hanged that, according to the duke, *'Les arbres commencent à se pencher sur les grands chemins du poids qu'on leur donne.'* ('The trees begin to lean over the highways from the weight that we add to them.')

Brittany in the Revolution
Intractable fiscal difficulties led Louis XVI to convene the Estates-General in May 1789. Deputies from Brittany were active in the events that followed. At the historic session of the National Assembly during the night of 4 August 1789, a Breton deputy, Guy Le Guen de Kérangal, helped to launch the wave of enthusiastic renunciation of feudal and seigneurial privileges with incisive mockery: *'Qu'on nous apporte ces titres qui obligent les hommes à passer les nuits à battre les étangs pour empêcher les grenouilles de troubler le sommeil de leurs voluptueux seigneurs!'* ('Bring us those deeds that oblige men to spend nights pounding ponds to prevent frogs from disturbing the sleep of their voluptuous lords!') The privileges that were abolished included those guaranteed to the Province of Brittany by the decrees of 1532. The province itself was abolished, along with its Parlement and Estates. France was divided into departments, including five in the territory of the former Province of Brittany. When regions were created in the 20th century, one of those Breton departments, Loire-Inférieure (today Loire-Atlantique), was excluded from the Region of Brittany – a decision that still rankles.

Many in Brittany welcomed the Revolution in its early days, but opposition grew in reaction to measures taken to control the Catholic Church, increased centralisation of power and the conscription of men to serve in the armies. Conflict between republicans and royalists led to a civil war called the Chouannerie – a sporadic succession of battles and guerrilla actions, including an unsuccessful British intervention in support of the royalists on the Quiberon peninsula in July 1795. Concessions to Catholic sentiment and military repression eventually ended the Chouannerie, but the cleavages within Breton society resulting from these conflicts endured into the 20th century.

Nineteenth-century Brittany
Brittany remained a predominantly agricultural society during the 19th century. Traditional farming began

slowly to modernise, for example with the introduction of machinery such as threshers. Linen production, once so prosperous, declined in the face of competition from the industrial manufacture of textiles in Britain and the north of France. Brittany's maritime commerce, disrupted by wars and blockades, did not recover its past glories. Intrepid Bretons did, however, continue to fish for cod off Newfoundland, and they extended their activities to the waters around Iceland.

Industries arose in some areas. Brest employed many workers in its naval shipyards. Fougères specialised in the manufacture of shoes, with 40 factories employing over 12,000 people by 1900. The modern method of preserving food in tins was developed in Nantes. Brittany became a leading producer of tinned sardines, finding markets as far away as California and Australia during their mid-century gold rushes. The construction of railway lines stimulated economic growth. In 1850, it took four days to travel from Paris to Nantes by stagecoach. The following year, a new railway line reduced that time to 13 hours.

Outsiders viewed Brittany, with its traditional agriculture and distinctive customs, as picturesque – but backward. When a railway line to Rennes was inaugurated in 1857, a weekly magazine, *L'Illustration*, opined that *'le passage [du premier train à grande vitesse] dans cette contrée classique de la superstition et de la sainte ignorance, va introduire les usages et les habitudes qui doivent faire bientôt rentrer la Bretagne dans le concert de notre civilisation'* ('the arrival of the first high-speed train in this classic land of superstition and holy ignorance will introduce customs and habits that should soon bring Brittany into the concert of our civilisation'). Many Bretons emigrated to cities outside Brittany (in particular, Paris) in search of opportunities that life on a farm did not offer. Bécassine, an early 20th-century cartoon character portraying a naïve Breton girl who works as a maid in Paris, reflected sophisticated society's condescending view of Brittany. Not coincidentally, Parisians discovered Brittany as an attractive holiday destination.

Meanwhile, Breton intellectuals were exploring and championing their cultural heritage. Théodore Hersart de La Villemarqué published *Barzaz Breiz* (Ballads of Brittany), a collection of legends, folk tales and music that he had gathered in lower (western) Brittany (1839). In later years, disputes arose over the authenticity of La Villemarqué's work, but he certainly contributed to growing respect for traditional Breton culture.

Others found inspiration in Brittany's dazzling landscapes and light to create art. A colony of innovative artists, including Émile Bernard and Paul Gauguin, gathered in Pont-Aven. You can admire views around Saint-Briac (Stage 5) that inspired Auguste Renoir, Paul Signac and others, or around Saint-Quay-Portrieux

(Stage 12), visited by Berthe Morisot and Eugène Boudin.

Most Bretons supported the monarchy through France's political upheavals during the 19th century. Deeply religious, they followed the teachings of the Catholic Church. Bretons expressed their religious faith solemnly in processions called *pardons* (which continue today as a tourist attraction as well as a religious ceremony). Pope Leo XIII urged French Catholics to accept the Third Republic in his encyclical *Au milieu des sollicitudes* (1892), but strife over the place of the Church in French society continued. In 1905, the historic law separating Church and State was enacted. This law and, in particular the inventories of Church property that it entailed, provoked anger in Brittany.

Early 20th-century Brittany
World War I began in July 1914. Some 600,000 Bretons served in the French armed forces during the war; more than 130,000 of them were killed. Pause, as you walk through a village, to look at the war memorial, with its list of names. The repetition of surnames highlights the tragedy of the war. In Paramé (Saint-Malo), a plaque on a street now called Rue des Six Frères Ruellan honours the memory of six brothers who were killed in the fighting.

Breton ports welcomed American soldiers after the United States entered the war in 1917. Among those soldiers was the African-American musician

James Reese Europe. His band, part of the 369th Infantry Regiment, introduced jazz to an appreciative public in France. When the band played the *Marseillaise* upon disembarking in Brest, they were surprised that the French soldiers and sailors present did not snap immediately to attention. It turned out that the French had not recognised the band's syncopated version of their national anthem.

Most Bretons continued after the war to live in rural communities. However, winds of change were blowing across Brittany… In 1924, the women who worked in Douarnenez's sardine canneries struck for an increase in their meagre wages. The owners brought in strike-breakers, provoking violence, but the women stood firm and finally prevailed after 48 days, winning an increase in their hourly wage from 0.80 to 1.00 franc.

The Depression of the 1930s affected the industrialised parts of Brittany more than the rural world. A small family farm would not prosper, of course, but it could survive. The hardships of unemployment and reductions in wages hit industrial workers hard. The workers in Fougères' shoe factories conducted a seven-month strike in 1932 that won concessions from the owners. Violent riots shook Brest in August 1935 as workers in the shipyards protested against austerity measures imposed by the government of Pierre Laval.

The legislative elections in 1936 were a triumph for the Popular Front, an electoral alliance of socialists, communists and radicals. While socialists and communists scored big gains elsewhere in France, conservative parties remained dominant in Brittany. Léon Blum's short-lived government disappointed its supporters, but it did implement important reforms – including one that people today still associate with the Popular Front: *congés payés* (paid holidays). Brittany became one of the favoured destinations of workers now able to go away on holiday.

International tensions and crises undermined Blum's government and its successors. Already in February 1937, Blum announced a 'pause' in the government's reforms, as credits were shifted to armaments. But France was unprepared for war when it came in September 1939 and, in particular, the German *Blitzkrieg* that quickly defeated the French armies in May–June 1940.

Brittany's location facing the Atlantic Ocean and its proximity to Great Britain gave the region strategic importance during the war. A German submarine arrived in Lorient on 7 July 1940, just two weeks after the armistice was signed. Lorient soon became an operational submarine base, followed by Brest and Saint-Nazaire. The Germans constructed fortified pens for their submarines, with concrete roofs up to 7.5m thick. Massive Allied bombing failed to destroy the pens but obliterated the port areas and caused

The GR34 trail snakes across the slope above the rocky coast (Stage 24)

many casualties among the French population.

The Resistance was active in Brittany during the war. Brave patriots gathered information about German military operations and conveyed it to British Intelligence. They smuggled people – in particular, Allied aircraft crew who had been shot down – out of France. The GR34 passes one of the beaches used for these operations: Plage Bonaparte (Stage 13). The Resistance also took direct action, most famously at Saint-Marcel where the Maquis fought a battle against German forces in June 1944.

Brittany after World War II

The tasks facing Bretons after the war were not merely reconstruction but also the transformation of their society. The most striking changes occurred in the rural world: a land of small, subsistence farms relying upon archaic methods became the leading agricultural region of France. Farms were consolidated into larger units, with extensive clearance of hedge rows. The adoption of modern equipment and methods increased production spectacularly. Livestock farming and meat packing have become a major sector of Brittany's economy. For example, 58% of the pigs raised in France in 2013 were Breton. Many of the farmers pushed off the land by the modernisation of agriculture found jobs in new factories (for example, Citroën in Rennes, 1961).

Modernisation has brought new challenges and harm to the environment. The heavy use of fertilisers to

Algal blooms at Binic: beautiful but unwelcome (Stage 12)

maximise agricultural production has put large quantities of nitrates into watercourses and groundwater. This pollution periodically produces algal blooms in the waters around some beaches. You will see signs that warn of *algues vertes* and the hydrogen sulphide (H_2S) that may be released by rotting algae.

Brittany, with its rocky coast lying along major sea lanes, has experienced terrible oil spills. A large portion of the *Torrey Canyon*'s 120,000 tons of crude oil, spilled after that supertanker struck Pollard's Rock between Cornwall and the Scilly Islands in 1967, drifted across the Channel and onto Breton beaches. The wreck of the *Amoco Cadiz* on the coast of Finistère in 1978 was even worse, as its cargo of 220,000 tons of crude oil polluted 300km of the Breton coast.

The transformation of Breton society since World War II, with its successes and vicissitudes, has instilled a new pride – a defiant rejection of feelings of inferiority that existed in the past. The publication in 1975 of Pierre-Jakez Hélias' memoir of traditional rural society, *Le Cheval d'orgueil* (The Horse of Pride), was a milestone in this evolution of mentalities. You will see the Breton flag everywhere: nine horizontal black and white stripes, representing the traditional dioceses, with an ermine canton, representing the Duchy. The role and influence of the Catholic Church declined during these years, and Breton politics shifted left. A poster created in 1981 by Alain Le Quernec illustrates these changes: Bécassine, no longer a timid maid, is portrayed as a fiery socialist militant, raising a

Bécassine as socialist militant, by Alain Le Quernec

clenched fist and shouting: *'Décidons chez nous'* – 'Decide for ourselves!'

CULTURE

Language

French is the main language of Brittany. This book includes a French–English glossary of words that are useful to know when walking along the coast (Appendix F). You will meet many people who speak at least some English, while an ability to converse in French will enrich your experience.

But what about Breton? The Britons who migrated to Armorica in the fourth–seventh centuries spoke a Celtic language, and they settled among people who spoke Gaulish (also a Celtic language). The Breton language developed in this society. Among modern Celtic languages, Breton is most closely related to Cornish and Welsh. By medieval times, Breton was the predominant language in lower Brittany, the region west of a line (roughly) between Saint-Brieuc and Vannes. In upper Brittany to the east of that line, people spoke Gallo, a Romance language related to French, a *langue d'oïl*. French, however, became the language of government and urban life throughout Brittany.

Breton was still widely spoken in lower Brittany on the eve of World War I, despite widespread disparagement (symbolised by Bécassine being drawn without a mouth) and official discrimination (pupils in state schools were forbidden to speak Breton and punished when they did so). More than a million people still spoke Breton in 1945, but the economic and social transformation of Brittany since then has marginalised the language. Only about 200,000 people now speak Breton (even fewer speak Gallo), and UNESCO classifies the language as 'severely endangered'. The Diwan Association seeks to reverse that trend; its schools offer immersive education in Breton to more than 4000 pupils. You are unlikely to hear the language spoken, but you may enjoy knowing a few words of Breton: *demat* (hello), *trugarez* (thank you), *kenavo* (goodbye).

Music and dance

The transformation of Breton society after 1945 could have marginalised traditional music and dance, just as the Breton language declined. This did not happen. Instead, Breton music has survived, evolved and flourished. Bretons adopted the Celtic harp and Highland bagpipes (larger than the traditional Breton bagpipe), and they formed bands (*bagadoù*; singular: *bagad*) modelled upon Scottish pipe bands. The French Navy's own, highly regarded *bagad*, Lann-Bihoué, was founded in 1952. An international bagpipe festival was held annually in Brest during the 1950–60s. The festival moved in 1971 and became the Festival Interceltique de Lorient, a hugely popular event with participants from all Celtic lands.

A new generation of musicians arrived in the 1960–70s. Alan Stivell, soon followed by others such as Dan Ar Braz, Gilles Servat and the group Tri Yann, led a renaissance of Celtic music, adopting modern themes and styles. On a more contemporary note, the Festival des Vieilles Charrues in Carhaix-Plouguer attracts big crowds with an eclectic mix of music (rock, rap, electro, folk, etc).

If you would like to experience Breton music and dance, look for a *fest-noz* (night festival). The *fest-noz* has roots in traditional village celebrations – at harvest time, for example – in which everyone danced, accompanied by singing and music played on bagpipes and bombardes. The *fest-noz* evolved after 1945, becoming popular in cities and among Bretons living outside Brittany. In 2012, it was inscribed on UNESCO's list of the Intangible Cultural Heritage of Humanity.

Food and drink

The food most closely associated with Brittany is the crêpe. Bretons distinguish between *galettes* – savoury pancakes made with buckwheat flour (*sarrasin*) – and *crêpes* – sweet pancakes made with white flour (*froment*). Menus offer innumerable fillings for these pancakes. The *galette complète* (ham, egg and grated cheese) is a good place to start – accompanied by a Breton cider. There are also fine beers brewed in Brittany that are appreciated by thirsty trekkers.

The north Breton coast is one of the leading areas for the cultivation (and consumption) of shellfish – in particular, oysters (*huîtres*), mussels (*moules*) and scallops (*coquilles Saint-Jacques*). You will see many rows of oyster racks and mussel stakes as you walk beside the coast. You may also see sheep grazing in meadows near Mont-Saint-Michel that are submerged during spring high tides. Salt-meadow lamb (*agneau de pré-salé*) is a local speciality.

The bread that is served with every meal will be accompanied by salted butter (*beurre demi-sel*). Bretons' preference for salted butter derives from the province's exemption from the salt tax during the Ancien

A galette complète; huîtres *(oysters)*; moules frites *(mussels with chips)*; coquilles Saint-Jacques *(scallops)*

Régime. Locally produced salt, being relatively cheap, was used to preserve butter. Should you prefer unsalted butter (*beurre doux*), it will also be available.

The GR34 passes through cities and larger towns where groceries and other supplies are readily available in supermarkets and speciality shops. Many towns have a weekly market in a central square where you can buy the ingredients for a fine picnic. Your options are more limited in small towns and villages: there may be a small grocer's shop (*épicerie*), but these have become rare in recent years. Bakeries (*boulangeries*) are more common, as French people prize a fresh baguette every day.

You can usually buy snacks such as a sandwich or quiche in a bakery. Bakeries generally open early in the morning (7 or 8am) and close for an hour or two at midday; they close in the evening at around 6 or 7pm.

WHEN TO GO

Your decision on when to go may be influenced by the weather. Brittany is reputed to be a rainy region, but Bretons will assure you: *'En Bretagne, il fait beau plusieurs fois par jour.'* ('In Brittany, the weather is fine several times a day.') You will win an appreciative smile from a Breton if you earnestly recite this witticism with the hint of an ironic wink. Indeed,

Brittany's climate is changeable. It does rain, but rarely all day. A rain shower may arrive suddenly – and then end as you put on your rain gear. You should definitely have that rain gear in your backpack, remembering that there's no such thing as bad weather, just the wrong clothes.

Brittany's weather is also moderate. Freezing temperatures and snow are rare in the winter. When the rest of France swelters during a summer heat wave, Bretons may enjoy temperatures in the mid 20s. However, the ocean does bring occasional storms which can be quite severe.

The Breton coast attracts many visitors during summer holidays, when some small towns become large ones: the population of Saint-Cast-le-Guildo, for example, increases from about 3400 permanent residents to over 30,000 in the summer. The influx of visitors generates animation in the area (many festivals are scheduled then, for example – see tourist information websites in Appendix E for further information) but may complicate the search for accommodation. There will, of course, be more people walking on the G34 during those summer months than other seasons.

Considering these factors, many consider the best seasons for hiking the GR34 to be late spring (May–June) and early autumn (September).

GETTING THERE AND AROUND

The most convenient way to travel to Mont-Saint-Michel is to take a bus operated by Keolis Armor from Rennes or Saint-Malo. Buses from Rennes, Saint-Malo and Pontorson take passengers to La Caserne, a commercial area (with a tourist office, hotels, campground, restaurants, gift shops and vast parking lots) on the mainland 2km south of Mont-Saint-Michel, where you'll find the first GR34 waymarks. There is rapid railway service (TGV) from Paris (Montparnasse station) to Rennes and Saint-Malo. Trains also run to Pontorson, linked to Mont-Saint-Michel by bus. Travel by ferry is another option: for those traveling from the UK, Brittany Ferries currently serves Saint-Malo from Portsmouth. There is also ferry service from Plymouth and Cork to Roscoff. In addition, Condor Ferries serves Saint-Malo from Poole (via the Channel Islands). If travelling by air to France, fly to Charles de Gaulle Airport (CDG), and then fly or take a train from Paris to Rennes. There is also railway service in other towns along the GR34: Dol-de-Bretagne, Saint-Brieuc, Paimpol, Lannion and Morlaix. Appendix D lists websites for these transport options.

There is extensive bus service within Brittany. BreizhGo operates inter-city lines that serve many towns along the GR34. In addition, bus lines radiate from principal cities: MAT (Saint-Malo), TUB (Saint-Brieuc), TILT (Lannion) and Linéotim (Morlaix). The

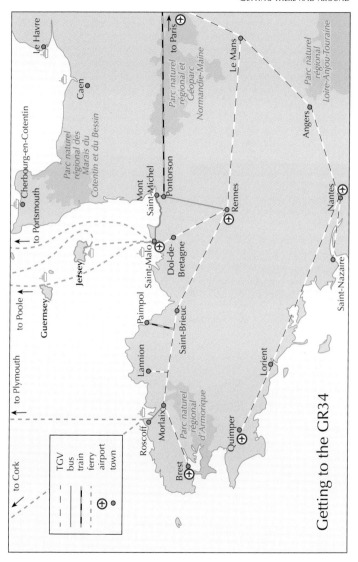

Getting to the GR34

information boxes at the beginning of each stage in this book identify bus lines that are useful for travel to or from one end of the stage, as well as lines that serve places along the route of a stage. All of these lines and the principal towns on the GR34 that they serve are listed in Appendix D, along with the bus companies' websites.

ACCOMMODATION

Options for accommodation are numerous on the north Brittany coast. There are many hotels and *chambres d'hôtes* (B&Bs), as well as a few *auberges de jeunesse* (youth hostels) and *gîtes d'étape* (similar to hostels), but they are unevenly distributed. (Note that the term *gîte* alone generally refers to a cottage that is rented

for a week or more.) The areas that attract the most tourists naturally have the most abundant and diverse supply of accommodation. Some hotels and many *chambres d'hôtes* close for a month or more during the winter, and most campsites are closed between autumn and early spring. There are numerous sources of information: in addition to commercial websites such as booking.com, airbnb.com, chambres-hotes.fr and bedand breakfast.eu, tourist office web-sites (Appendix E) include lists of accommodation.

Camping is an attractive option for hardy trekkers. There are many campgrounds close to the coast. They cater principally to campers who travel by car or bicycle but welcome back-packers as well. A few campgrounds

Chambres d'hôtes *and* crêperie *in Le Yaudet (Stage 22)*

offer overnight accommodation for trekkers without camping gear. Some backpackers also camp wild (*camping sauvage* or *bivouac*). Wild camping is not officially authorised in most places, but campers who are discreet (setting up a light tent in the evening and striking it in the morning) generally have no difficulties. The logistics (finding a good pitch for the tent, etc) can be complicated, but campers on the GR34 are quite positive about their experience.

Appendix C provides a list of selected accommodation, focusing on hotels and *chambres d'hôtes* on sections of the GR34 where accommodation is sparse, as well as establishments that provide a warm welcome to trekkers. Also listed are youth hostels and campgrounds offering accommodation for trekkers.

All such lists are snapshots in time, subject to change. It is advisable to book accommodation in advance to avoid unpleasant surprises. In some places there may be only one hotel or a single *chambres d'hôtes*. If it has no vacancy when you arrive without a reservation (or has simply closed), you might have a long walk to the next place.

CLOTHING AND EQUIPMENT

While Brittany enjoys a moderate climate, you should be prepared for inclement weather: it would be unusual to walk far along the GR34 without encountering wind and rain. It is important to stay warm and dry in those conditions. Footwear depends on individual preference. While a few sections of the trail are quite rocky, most walkers will be comfortable in sturdy low-cut shoes, rather than heavy hiking boots. Many people use trekking poles on these trails (with rubber tips where appropriate). You can travel light on the GR34, since you can spend each night under a roof if you wish. It is easy to hand-wash clothes in most places – but it may be helpful to have a flat, rubber stopper for the sink in your room. If you anticipate spending nights in campgrounds that offer accommodation to trekkers, bring a sleeping bag liner (a *sac à viande*) and a light towel.

The basic trekking kit in a medium-sized backpack should work well for you. Cicerone's article with tips for trek packing provides useful guidance: www.cicerone.co.uk/top-tips-for-european-trek-packing.

WAYMARKING

Your lodestar on the GR34 will be the standard GR mark – a pair of rectangles, white over red – painted on trees, rocks, buildings, fence posts, etc. Two white strokes under the GR mark, joined in an inverted L, signal a turn. An X formed by white and red strokes indicates an incorrect route. You will also see many signs that indicate distances or times to places along the trail. The GR34 is generally well marked, thanks to the efforts of local authorities and volunteers.

GR mark for right turn (Stage 8)

MAPS

France's Institut national de l'information géographique et forestière (IGN) publishes an excellent series of topographical maps: TOP25 (1:25,000). Eight TOP25 maps cover the 28 stages of the GR34 described in this book. The information at the beginning of each stage includes the relevant TOP25 reference(s). IGN also publishes a map for the entire route covered by this book: *Sentier des Douaniers Bretagne Nord* (1:100,000). All of these maps show the route of the GR34.

IGN's digital app, Cartes IGN Liberté, includes maps of different scales on which you can mark routes. It is sold as an annual subscription. A similar app, iPhiGéNie, also uses IGN maps, but offers fewer features than Cartes IGN Liberté and is slightly cheaper. Both of these apps show your position on the map. If you use one of these apps, which can zoom to large scale, you may not need the TOP25 maps; you could manage with a smaller-scale paper map.

The Fédération Française de la Randonnée Pédestre publishes 'topoguides' for hiking trails in France. These guides, in French, include maps, descriptions of the route and practical information. Three topoguides cover the section of the GR34 described in this book.

Appendix E provides names and websites for purchasing maps.

In addition, note that GPX tracks for the routes in this guidebook are available to download free at www. cicerone.co.uk/1061/GPX. A GPS device is an excellent aid to navigation, but you should also carry a map (paper and/or digital) and compass and know how to use them. GPX files are provided in good faith, but neither the author nor the publisher accepts responsibility for their accuracy.

MONEY

The currency of France is the euro (€). Most businesses accept payment by credit card, but there are exceptions. Some *chambres d'hôtes*, for example, require payment in cash or by cheque (drawn upon a French bank). There are banks and post offices with ATMs (*distributeurs automatiques de billets*) in many, but not all, of the towns along the GR34.

STAYING IN TOUCH

Mobile telephone networks cover the entire Brittany coast, but the strength of the signal will vary. A 2017 EU directive barred roaming charges for European mobile telephone services. This directive no longer applies to the UK, post-Brexit, so UK telephone operators may reinstate roaming charges for travel within the EU.

Wireless internet service (WiFi) is usually available in hotels, *chambres d'hôtes*, and campgrounds. In cities, many cafés and restaurants offer WiFi to their customers, as do train stations.

HEALTH AND SAFETY

There are fewer risks to your health and safety on the GR34 than, for example, crossing a 2500m pass in the Alps. There are, however, some sections of the trail traversing steep slopes that are exposed. While Brittany's climate is moderate, major storms sometimes sweep in from the ocean. If the sky suddenly darkens and the wind picks up, avoid high, exposed ground and seek shelter. The coming storm could be intense, with lightning.

Carry a basic first aid kit, and exercise ordinary caution and foresight. Be aware of the risk of ticks (vectors of Lyme disease). It is advisable to check for ticks after walking through high grass and bushes.

EU citizens and residents should obtain and carry a European Health Insurance Card (EHIC). For UK citizens and residents, the EHIC has been replaced by the Global Health Insurance Card (GHIC) and the 'UK EHIC' – see www.nhs.uk for details of how to apply. Supplemental personal insurance may be worthwhile. Some walking associations (such as the Club Alpin Français) offer optional insurance with membership.

The standard European number for emergency services is: 112.

USING THIS GUIDE

This guidebook presents the GR34 between Mont-Saint-Michel and Roscoff in 28 stages that correspond to

A trekker on the coast southwest of Pointe du Grouin (Stage 3)

daily walks. They range in length from 12.5km (a short walk, leaving time to explore a town) to 32.5km (a longer walk that could be broken into two stages). Basic information is given at the beginning of each stage: start and end points, distance, total ascent and descent, walking time, maps, places where refreshments may be available, public transport and accommodation. After a summary of highlights, there is a detailed description of the walk, including points of interest. Intermediate times from the starting point are given within the text. All times are approximate. You will learn to estimate your own walking times in relation to the 'guide times' as you progress. There are 1:100,000 maps showing the route for each stage, supplemented by 1:40,000 and 1:25,000 maps of selected urban areas. Places or features on the maps that are mentioned in the route description are highlighted in the text in **bold** to aid orientation.

There are five appendices: A provides several itineraries on the GR34 to fit into a week's holiday; B comprises a route planner that lists where facilities are available; C lists accommodation; D provides transport information; E lists other useful contacts; and F offers useful phrases and a French–English glossary for coastal walking.

Bonne route!

THE BRITTANY COAST PATH

The GR34 follows the coast between Beg an Fry and Beg Gracia (Stage 24)

STAGE 1
Mont-Saint-Michel to Saint-Broladre

Start	Mont-Saint-Michel (La Caserne)
Finish	Saint-Broladre
Distance	19.5km
Ascent	185m
Descent	175m
Time	5hr
Map	IGN TOP25 1215OT
Refreshments	Cafés/restaurants in Quatre Salines, Roz-sur-Couesnon, Saint-Broladre
Transport	Keolis Armor buses from Rennes and Saint-Malo to Mont-Saint-Michel/La Caserne; Pontorson–Mont-Saint-Michel/La Caserne shuttle bus; BreizhGo line 17 (summer)
Accommodation	Hotels and/or *chambres d'hôtes* in Quatre Salines, Roz-sur-Couesnon, Saint-Marcan, Saint-Broladre; campground in Roz-sur-Couesnon

The GR34 trekker may feel an affinity with the pilgrims who walked to Mont-Saint-Michel over the centuries. This stage offers iconic views of this UNESCO World Heritage site before the trail turns west to follow the coast on a long, level dyke. The latter part of the stage moves inland and is no longer so flat. The route enters forests and crosses hills, with intervals of open land offering views over Mont-Saint-Michel Bay. Finishing on a narrow, winding trail through the wooded Riskop Valley, you could almost forget that you are anywhere near the sea.

Our trek along the GR34 begins in Normandy beside Mont-Saint-Michel Bay at **La Caserne**, a commercial area (with a tourist office, hotels, campground, restaurants, gift shops and vast parking lots) on the mainland 2km south of Mont-Saint-Michel. (While the official starting point of the GR34 is Mont-Saint-Michel itself, the GR marks that

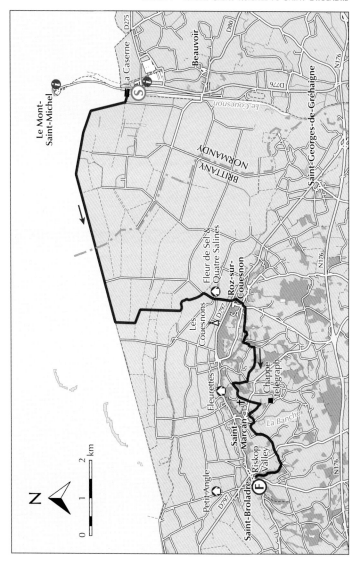

A rainbow beside Mont-Saint-Michel augurs well for a trek along the GR34

you will follow along the Breton coast begin here.) The conical form of Mont-Saint-Michel presides majestically over the flat landscape and sea.

MONT-SAINT-MICHEL

In AD708, Archangel Michael appeared in a dream to Aubert, Bishop of Avranches, and commanded him to build a sanctuary dedicated to the archangel on a nearby island. Aubert did not comply, even after the archangel repeated the command in a second dream. Finally, after a third dream, during which the archangel stressed the point by poking his finger into Aubert's skull, the bishop wisely complied with the command. (A skull with a hole in it is preserved as a relic of Saint Aubert in the Saint-Gervais Basilica of Avranches.) The sanctuary was dedicated to Saint Michael in 709, and the island became known as Mont-Saint-Michel. A chapel called Notre-Dame-sous-Terre was built in the 10th century, followed by a Romanesque church in the 11–12th centuries. The Gothic abbey that crowns the island was built during the 13–16th centuries, with the spire and its golden statue of Saint Michael added in 1897.

Modern constructions – a causeway linking Mont-Saint-Michel to the mainland (1877) and a dam across the Couesnon (1969) – interfered with the flow of water around the bay and permitted silt to accumulate. Mont-Saint-Michel was no longer an island. Works to make Mont-Saint-Michel an island again and to keep it that way were completed in 2015. A new dam on the Couesnon increases the flow of water carrying sediment into the bay, and the replacement of the causeway by a bridge allows water to flow freely around the island.

This drainage canal marks the border between Normandy and Brittany

The new dam includes a graceful bridge: cross the bridge, heading west, and continue to a line of trees, where you will see a GR mark on a post. Turn right here and enjoy a magnificent view of Mont-Saint-Michel as you walk north on a dyke for 1km. The trail then turns left.

Continue for 6.5km along the dyke between cultivated polder lands on the left and grasslands on the right where salt-meadow sheep graze. Take care to avoid stepping in small rabbit holes that may be concealed by high grass. One of the drainage canals that you pass is the unmarked **border** between two departments, Manche and Ille-et-Vilaine: welcome to Brittany!

Turn left on a dyke where a sign points to Roz-sur-Couesnon (**1hr 45min**). ▶ Turn left after 500 metres and then right 400 metres further on. Continue straight to reach a T-junction with a bicycle path, where a left turn is clearly marked. Upon reaching a road, turn right and pass a hamlet called **Quatre Salines**. Cross a main road and follow a smaller road that climbs toward Roz-sur-Couesnon. After 100 metres on this road, where it makes a hairpin right turn, leave the road to the left and then immediately turn right to climb a steep, narrow trail. ▶ Turn left where the trail levels off and enter **Roz-sur-Couesnon** (**3hr**).

Walk through the village: right at a T-junction, left where the road forks, left on Rue de la Margasse and finally right on Rue de la Bossette, which leads out of

A variant continues straight along the dyke to La Châtellier, where it rejoins the GR34. Its length is 14.5km, compared with 30km by the main route. It is unsigned but easy to navigate.

A sign here warns walkers to be careful on this 'difficult and slippery' path: 'Prudence! Sentier difficile et glissant'.

town. After 750 metres the GR34 turns left on a narrow trail into the woods. Descend to a footbridge over a stream, then climb a slope with steps. Where the trail levels off it follows a sunken road to the right (northwest). Turn left at a T-junction with a surfaced road and right on a trail back into the forest.

After emerging from the forest, turn left to walk past a group of houses and left at another T-junction. Turn right after 50 metres on a dirt road that rises toward the woods and eventually crests at about 80m elevation. The land opens and offers a view over the sea to the north.

Continue for 1km, cross a road and follow a dirt road to the right (north) into the woods. The road leads to a T-junction with a small road. Follow that road to the left and cross a road where there is an old stone **cross**. Continue straight on what is now a dirt path toward Le Télégraphe.

The path climbs gently: turn right where it levels off. (Going straight here leads to a restored **Chappe telegraph**.) ◄ Descend 300 metres to a T-junction on the edge of **Saint-Marcan**. The GR34 continues to the left here on Le Couronel toward Saint-Broladre (**4hr 15min**).

The road curves left and enters the woods above Saint-Marcan. Cross a road and continue on a road that curves uphill to the right. (A sign points to Le Vieux Moulin.) Just before the crest of the hill, turn left on a dirt path. Follow this pleasant trail between stone walls to a T-junction with a road, where you turn left. Walk along this quiet road for about a kilometre, crossing a main road along the way.

Opposite a pond, turn right on a trail that descends into the woods through the beautiful **Riskop Valley** to Saint-Broladre. The GR34 does not enter the centre of Saint-Broladre, but instead turns left behind its church and climbs a dirt path. Continue straight past the church for accommodation, restaurants and shops in **Saint-Broladre**.

Chappe telegraphs, first built in the 1790s, formed a network of semaphore signalling stations that were used until supplanted in the mid 19th century by the electric telegraph.

STAGE 2
Saint-Broladre to Cancale

Start	Saint-Broladre
Finish	Cancale
Distance	30.5km
Ascent	310m
Descent	320m
Time	7hr 30min
Map	IGN TOP25 1215OT
Refreshments	Cafés/restaurants in Mont-Dol, Hirel, Saint-Benoît-des-Ondes, Cancale
Transport	BreizhGo line 17 (summer); railway service in Dol-de-Bretagne (1km)
Accommodation	Hotels and/or *chambres d'hôtes* in Mont-Dol, Dol-de-Bretagne, Hirel, Saint-Benoît-des-Ondes, Cancale; youth hostel in Cancale

Mont-Saint-Michel Bay comes back into view as you emerge from forests and complete your crossing of high ground during the first part of this stage. The trail descends to lower, flat terrain – with a bump over Mont-Dol. After Hirel, the GR34 follows an arc along the coast to Cancale, a city famous for its oysters.

This stage begins behind the church in **Saint-Broladre**: walk up the Impasse du Donjon, a steep gravel path, to a road. Turn left, pass a cemetery and immediately turn right to walk up steps to another road. Turn right and follow the road downhill to the main road (**D80**). ▶

Turn left and walk 100 metres along the D80; then turn left to follow a dirt road that rises into a forest. Continue straight, passing a smaller trail on the right, and then turn right on a trail beside a sign for the 'Monument de Tréal'. This is a delightful, rolling trail in the forest.

If you spent the night in the *chambres d'hôtes* north of the village, you can walk back to the centre, turn right on the D80 and rejoin the GR34 here.

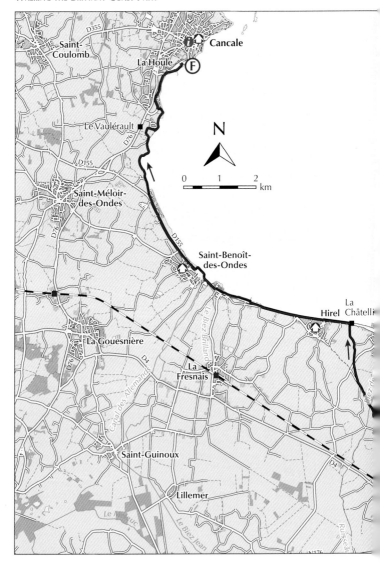

The trail emerges from the forest and reaches a T-junction with a surfaced road. Turn right and walk across an open plateau. Continue straight through a crossroads at **Tertre Hubault**. The road descends to a T-junction: turn left and immediately right on a road (direction: La Ville Guillaume). Turn right on a dirt trail after 700 metres.

The trail leaves the woods, offering a broad view north toward the bay, and descends to a T-junction with a small road. A sign points left to a 'Site Mégalithique' (a small group of Neolithic stones called Outre-Tombes), but the GR34 turns right. After 250 metres, turn left to descend a dirt road (marked 'GR34 Cancale'). Cross a main road at a hamlet called **l'Epinay** and continue straight on what is now a surfaced road (**1hr 15min**).

Cross a small stone bridge over a canal called **la Banche** and turn left on a dirt path. Continue across fields

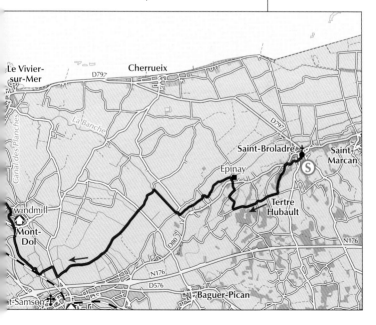

and through a group of farm buildings to a T-junction with a road beside a bridge. Turn right here and walk along this road. After 50 metres, where the road curves right, turn left on a smaller road and then immediately right (just before a bridge) on a grass path. Walk beside a small drainage canal to a T-junction with a surfaced road. Turn left to cross the canal on a bridge. A sign points the way to Mont-Dol, and indeed, the wooded mound of Mont-Dol is visible in the distance.

The GR34 now follows a dirt road beside another canal for almost 4km, crossing a road along the way. While Mont-Dol draws closer on your right, Saint-Samson Cathedral of Dol-de-Bretagne emerges above the trees ahead. Near the end of this walk (approaching a main road), cross the canal and continue in the same direction on the other side.

Upon reaching the road, turn right and then, after 300 metres beside this busy road, turn left on a small road, marked 'GR34 Cancale'. Pass a water treatment plant on the left and curve to the right where a trail branches left and passes under a railway line. The GR34 continues towards Mont-Dol, while the side-trail leads to Dol-de-Bretagne – a town with all facilities.

DOL-DE-BRETAGNE

Samson was one of the Founder Saints of Brittany. Born in South Wales, he was ordained as a bishop around AD521. Samson founded Dol in the mid sixth century. (The town's name was changed to Dol-de-Bretagne in the 20th century.) The great Saint-Samson Cathedral attests to the importance of the bishopric in the Middle Ages.

Dol makes a brief appearance in the Bayeux Tapestry: William (Duke of Normandy), Harold (Earl of Wessex) and a Norman army besieged Conan (Duke of Brittany) in Dol's motte-and-bailey castle. Conan escaped by sliding down a rope, as depicted on the tapestry ('*ET VENERUNT AD DOL ET CONAN FUGA VERTIT*' – 'and they came to Dol and Conan turned in flight'). His pursuers finally caught Conan in Dinan: the tapestry shows him surrendering the city's keys on the end of a lance ('*ET CUNAN CLAVES PORREXIT*' – 'and Conan passed out the keys').

Dol was the ancestral home of Scotland's House of Stuart.

Continue on the road leading to Mont-Dol. Turn right at a T-junction and walk up to the town. After the road turns left, cross a park on the right and climb steps to another road. Turn right and continue straight to reach the Place de l'Église in the centre of **Mont-Dol** (**3hr**).

The Moulin du Tertre atop Mont-Dol still functions with its original machinery

> **Mont-Dol** is a rounded mound composed principally of granite, with a broad vein of dolerite running through it. Evidence of a Neanderthal settlement or hunting camp has been found on the southeast side of the mound, with bones of animals they hunted (including mammoths, woolly rhinoceros, bison, cave lions and bears).

Turn left on Rue de l'Église Saint-Pierre. Walk a short distance, then turn right and walk in front of the town hall (*mairie*) to climb a steep (*escarpé*) trail. After passing two old **windmills** you reach a clearing where there is a tower (offering a 360-degree view of the surrounding area and Mont-Saint-Michel Bay from its roof) and a chapel that was originally a Chappe semaphore station. A sign beside a large rock on the edge of the clearing refers to a legend about Saint-Michel fighting Satan. ▶

As Saint-Michel triumphantly flung the devil off Mont-Dol, Satan clawed desperately at this rock, leaving grooves that are visible today.

45

The GR34 descends from Mont-Dol on a steep trail. At the bottom, turn left on a road and then right. After 700 metres, turn left on a side road. A short distance further, turn right at a T-junction, cross a main road, continue on a small road and then turn right on a quiet road into the country.

Continue straight where your dirt road joins a surfaced road. At a fork, bear right on a dirt road and continue straight past a road on the right (350 metres from the fork). After another 150 metres, dogleg right/left across a main road and continue north on a smaller road. About 5km from Mont-Dol, you reach the coast. Mont-Saint-Michel is visible on the eastern horizon. ◄ Turn left toward Hirel, 1km away, and walk on a path outside the dyke that is reserved for walkers and cyclists (**4hr 30min**).

The GR34 follows the coast on a big arc from **Hirel**: first northwest to **Saint-Benoît-des-Ondes** (4.5km from Hirel), then curving north and northeast to reach Cancale. You pass several cylindrical stone buildings with conical roofs: former windmills, some converted into homes. On the right, there are numerous warehouses and basins devoted to raising oysters. A vending machine sells oysters 24 hours a day. ◄

About 500 metres after the 24hr vending machine, the GR34 branches right on a small gravel road close to the seashore. Bear right at a T-junction with a paved road, following a sign that points to Vauléraut and Cancale. (A sign points to the left for a high-tide route.) The road leads to a beach, where you walk a short distance to stairs on the left to a trail above the beach.

After a brief passage through woods, the trail reaches open country. It's a delightful walk: fields on the left, trees on the right, and the sea with the sound of waves below. The trail descends to a small cove. Walk a short distance on the beach here, then climb a trail that returns to the woods beside a beautiful, ivy-covered stone house.

The trail levels off where it emerges from the woods and passes a group of large stone buildings. Continue north on a dirt road, and less than 50 metres after passing a château (**Le Vaulérault**), turn right onto another dirt

The variant trail that you passed during Stage 1 joins the main trail here at a place called La Châtellier.

Buying oysters from a vending machine may bring to mind Jonathan Swift's comment: 'He was a brave man who first ate an oyster.'

road (**6hr 45min**). Descend through a neighbourhood of large homes and gardens to reach a broad, grassy area overlooking the sea. A sign announces sternly that this is private property where camping and picnics are prohibited – but you can still appreciate the magnificent view over the emerald sea, and you do have the right to walk here. The GR34 follows a public right of way along the coast, established by law.

Follow a broad, smooth path that first curves to the left and then traces the coast above the sea. ▶ The path becomes a narrow trail near the edge of the cliff, turns left and climbs steeply to a road. Turn right and walk beside the road. Pass La Ferme Marine, which offers exhibits and guided tours about the cultivation of oysters. The road leads through **La Houle** to **Cancale**, an animated town with numerous cafés/restaurants and accommodation.

Cancale's oyster fields are well guarded

If the weather is sunny, you will see why this is called the Emerald Coast.

STAGE 3
Cancale to La Guimorais

Start	Cancale
Finish	La Guimorais
Distance	22km
Ascent	860m
Descent	845m
Time	5hr 45min
Map	IGN TOP25 1116ET
Refreshments	Café/restaurants at Port-Picain, Port-Mer, Pointe du Grouin, Plage du Verger, La Guimorais
Transport	MAT Line 9 (summer)
Accommodation	Hotel at Pointe de Grouin; a *chambres d'hôtes* in La Guimorais

This stage presents some of the most spectacular scenery of the entire Breton coast. The first section, from Cancale to Pointe du Grouin, is pleasant without being memorable. Then, after you round the headland, the GR34 offers 14km of dramatic coastal walking: steep cliffs and rocky shores alternating with sandy beaches.

A bust of Daniel de La Touche (1570–1635) commemorates the founder of a short-lived French colony in Brazil, Saint-Louis de Maragnan – today's São Luís.

From **Cancale**, pick up the GR34 on Quai Gambetta, where numerous restaurants face the bay. Walk north-east on a boardwalk and turn left beside the lighthouse at **Pointe de Crolles**. ◀ On a clear day, Mont-Saint-Michel and Mont-Dol are visible on the horizon.

The route follows a hairpin left turn up a road and branches right on a dirt path. Pass a war memorial that includes statues of both a soldier and a sailor. Offshore, you will see numerous rows of oyster racks, emerging from the sea as the tide ebbs or submerged by the rising tide.

Continue along the littoral path, often with a wall on the left and a cliff (with protective fence) on the right, with views over the bay. Opposite the **Pointe de la**

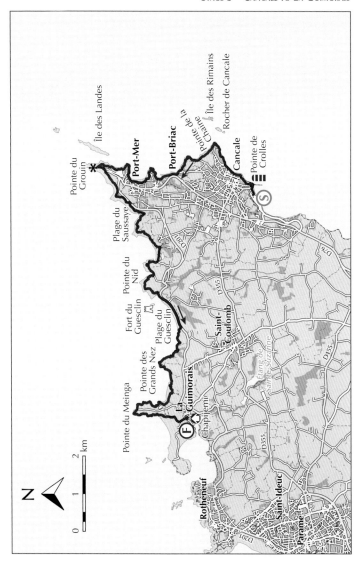

OYSTERS

In 1545, King François I granted Cancale the status of *ville* (city) in recognition of the quality of its *huîtres* (oysters). In 2019, the production of Cancale oysters was declared to be part of France's *patrimoine culturel immatériel* (intangible cultural heritage). Cancale's oysters experienced many vicissitudes and transformations between those two dates. Excessive harvesting and parasites decimated stocks; regulation and the introduction of new varieties restored stocks. Today, France produces 82% of Europe's oysters – and the French eat most of them.

The oysters begin life as larvae in the waters of the Atlantic coast. When the larvae have grown to become *naissains* (spat), they are transported to Cancale. *Huîtres creuses* (hollow oysters) are placed in mesh bags upon racks that are alternately covered and exposed by the tides; *huîtres plates* (flat oysters) grow upon the sea bed. The oysters are harvested after 3–4 years. The *ostréiculteurs* (oyster farmers) are not idle during this time, as they tend the bags of *huîtres creuses*, turning them over periodically.

Chaine, two rocky islands stand close offshore: Rocher de Cancale and Île des Rimains. The path descends to beaches – **Port-Briac**, Port-Picain, **Port-Mer** – and climbs to traverse forests across the steep slope.

The GR34 reaches **Pointe du Grouin** in open country, passing a coastal surveillance station (*sémaphore*) and a World War II bunker (**2hr**). ◄ The route turns back beside the bunker (just before a path leading to a map table and the extremity of the headland) and returns to its coastal path above the cliffs, leaving the tourist infrastructure behind.

The island offshore, Île-des-Landes, is a bird sanctuary; posters inside the bunker describe the birds and other wildlife of this area.

The GR34 now follows the coast southwest through mostly open country, offering fantastic views over cliffs that drop to boulders along the shore. Continually climbing and descending, the rocky path is a challenge, but it is well marked and easy to follow. In a few places, the slope beside the trail drops precipitously, so you must concentrate on your footing.

Along the way, beautiful crescents of sand interrupt the rocky shore, and side-trails give access to the beaches. **Plage du Saussaye**, 2.5km from Pointe du Grouin, is a

*Fort du Guesclin
at low tide*

good place to pause for a picnic lunch. One kilometre further, you may find snacks being sold beside Plage du Verger. A short side-trail near Pointe des Daules leads to a *corps de garde*, a small stone building that sheltered those responsible for surveillance of the coast – one of many built at intervals along the Sentier des Douaniers.

Walk past the small Plage du Petit Port and around **Pointe du Nid**: Fort du Guesclin on its island close to the shore appears dramatically. The trail descends to **Plage du Guesclin (3hr 45min)**; walk on the path beside the beach. Near the end of the beach, walk up steps and continue beside a road. After just 50 metres, turn right on a trail that goes around **Pointe des Grands Nez**, leading to Plage de la Touesse.

Walk along this beach to the large spur of rock that divides it and climb the stairs. The trail descends on the other side of this rock, but remains above the beach. Soon, the trail turns right to lead you around another headland, **Pointe du Meinga (5hr 15min)**. The path is not so smooth here, but the views are breathtaking. ▶

Pointe du Grouin, nearly 7km to the east, is visible.

The path along the western side of Pointe du Meinga is somewhat smoother. As you approach a beach, watch for a GR mark indicating a left turn (1km after the Pointe). The turn takes you uphill to a grassy field. Continue on a dirt path into the woods and then a surfaced road in a residential area, Impasse des Nielles. Turn left at a T-junction to walk into **La Guimorais**. A hairpin right turn on Impasse du Moulin de la Mer leads to a *chambres d'hôtes*.

STAGE 4
La Guimorais to Saint-Malo

Start	La Guimorais (Impasse du Moulin de la Mer)
Finish	Saint-Malo (Porte Saint-Vincent)
Distance	12.5km
Ascent	180m
Descent	195m
Time	3hr 30min
Map	IGN TOP25 1116ET
Refreshments	Cafés/restaurants in Rothéneuf, Saint-Malo
Transport	MAT Line 9; railway, bus and ferry service in Saint-Malo
Accommodation	Hotels, *chambres d'hôtes*, youth hostel in Saint-Malo

The GR34 continues along the coast to reach a great Breton city: Saint-Malo. The scenery along this path is not so dramatic as the previous stage, but it is a pleasant, easy walk. This short stage allows time to visit Saint-Malo, walking around the ramparts and exploring the city's maze of narrow streets.

In **La Guimorais**, Impasse du Moulin de la Mer leads a small cove, Anse du Lupin. There are two options here, depending on the state of the tide.

These oak logs form a breakwater that has protected Saint-Malo's Grande Plage du Sillon for 200 years: about 500 of the 1000 logs were replaced in 2021–2022

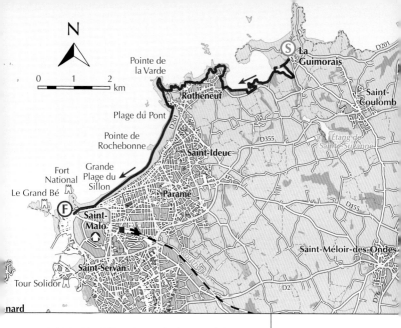

At high tide, follow the marked route of the GR34, which turns left on a narrow trail at the edge of the cove. The trail passes through dense vegetation and pine trees, then descends to reach a dyke. Cross this dyke and walk up to a path beside a field, with a steep slope on the right.

About 300 metres after the dyke, a GR mark points to a right turn down the slope. However, the trail from here down the slope is steep and difficult. Continue instead 40 metres further to a small trail on the right that descends gently in the woods to the beach. A GR mark on a tree 10 metres after the turn confirms that this is the right choice. At the bottom of the trail, turn left to walk along the beach.

Low-tide variant

At low tide, you can cross the cove on a more direct line: turn right at the cove and follow a trail beside the shore to the ruins of an old dyke. There is a clear path across this dyke through the seaweed that covers it. Cross the dyke and continue to the right along the beach. Soon you will see GR marks on the rocks bordering the beach, indicating that you have rejoined the GR34.

Walk a short distance to a road that comes down to the beach. Leave the beach on this road and immediately turn right on a path beside a forest. The trail follows the coast around a small promontory and then an inlet in a wooded area. Turn right on a road and walk 300 metres to a dirt road that leads to a beach. A 500-metre walk on this beach brings you to **Rothéneuf** (**1hr**).

> **Jacques Cartier**, born in Saint-Malo, explored the Gulf of St Lawrence and the St Lawrence River during three historic voyages in search of a Northwest Passage to Asia (1534–1542). Aboriginal guides told Cartier about a route up the river to *kanata*, a Huron-Iroquois word for 'village'. They were referring to a village at the site of the present-day city of Québec, but Cartier later used the word 'Canada' to describe the area around that village; he also called the St Lawrence River the *'rivière du Canada'* – and the name expanded from there… After his voyages, Cartier bought a country home near Rothéneuf called Limoëlou, which now houses the Jacques Cartier Museum.

The Rochers Sculptés portray historical figures carved in granite by Abbé Fouré (1839–1910), a deaf, speech-impaired man who expressed himself eloquently in sculpture.

Easily accessible from nearby Saint-Malo, this is a popular area for family outings.

Leave the beach and walk up Rue du Havre. Turn right after 100 metres (or continue straight for the commercial centre). Upon reaching Rue de la Roche, turn right, then left on Allée Notre Dame des Flots. Follow the marked path, passing the entrance to the Rochers Sculptés. ◄

The coastal path curves across a steep slope to reach a road in a residential area. After a short walk, descend steps on the right to follow a path between majestic houses and Plage du Val. Turn right on Avenue du Nicet, which curves left. At a T-junction, shaded by tall pine trees, turn right and walk 100 metres to a cul-de-sac. A gap in the hedges here leads to a path: turn right and descend stairs to reach a trail that winds along the coast through open country to **Pointe de la Varde** (**2hr 15min**). ◄

After rounding the headland, walk southeast past old fortifications. At the base of this peninsula, pass a traffic barrier and follow a road into a residential area. Descend steps on the right and turn left to walk along a dyke that leads to **Plage du Pont**.

The GR34 follows a succession of beaches from here to Saint-Malo: Minihic, Rochebonne, Hoguette, Sillon – a distance of about 5km. You can walk on the sand or on embankments most of the way, apart from a short section that follows streets inland from **Pointe de Rochebonne**. Finally, you reach the ramparts of **Saint-Malo**. Pass through **Porte Saint-Vincent** to enter the city within the ramparts (*intra-muros*).

SAINT-MALO

Saint-Malo prospered in the 16–17th centuries as one of Europe's greatest ports. Its sailors fished in the waters around Newfoundland for cod, which they sold in the Mediterranean. They carried exports of Breton products, such as linen, hemp and salt, and returned with wine and vegetable oils. Sailors from Saint-Malo named a group of islands in the South Atlantic the 'Malouines'; the Spanish version of that name was 'Malvinas', but the British called them the 'Falklands'. Saint-Malo's ships were active in wartime, especially during wars against Britain and the Netherlands from the late 17th century into the early 19th century. The French waged *guerre de course* (commerce raiding) with *corsaires* (privateers) authorised by letters of marque. While historians question the strategic value of privateering, Saint-Malo proclaims itself the 'Cité Corsaire' and celebrates the memory of two Malouin privateers in particular: René Duguay-Trouin (1673–1736), whose valorous deeds won him a commission in the French Navy, and Robert-Charles Surcouf (1773–1827), who earned enough as a privateer (and slave trader) to own ships and retire as a prosperous landowner.

Saint-Malo is an interesting place to visit. Walk around the ramparts and observe the 17th-century Fort National and the Île du Grand Bé (site of the tomb of Chateaubriand, a famous 19th-century author), which can be reached on foot at low tide. The Museum of History and Ethnography is housed beside Porte Saint-Vincent. Those interested in maritime history can visit the Étoile du Roy, a replica of an 18th-century privateer frigate, and the Cape Horner Museum (Musée du Long Cours Cap Hornier) in the Tour Solidor.

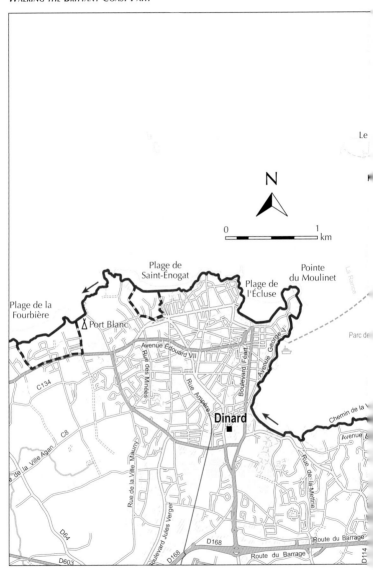

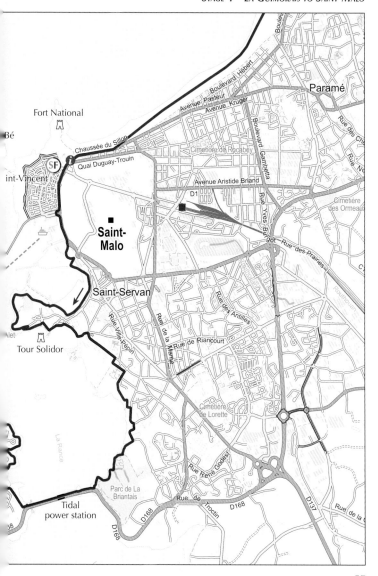

Paramé

Fort National

Bé

Chaussée du Sillon

SF

Quai Duguay-Trouin

int-Vincent

Avenue Pasteur

Avenue Kruger

Boulevard Hébert

Boulevard Gambetta

Cimetière de Rocabey

Avenue Aristide Briand

D1

Rue Yves-Burgot—Rue des Prairies—

Rue des Ch

Rue No

Cimetière
des Ormeau

Saint-
Malo

Saint-Servan

Rue des Antilles

Rue de Riancourt

Rue de la Marne

Rue Ville-Pépin

Alet

Tour Solidor

Cimetière
de Lorette

Rue René Godest

Rue de Troctin

Parc de La
Briantais

D168

D168

D137

D168

Rue de la

La Rance

Tidal
power station

38

STAGE 5
Saint-Malo to Lancieux

Start	Saint-Malo (Porte Saint-Vincent)
Finish	Lancieux (centre)
Distance	20km via 'sea bus' crossing to Dinard (+13.5km around Rance estuary)
Ascent	485m (+340m around Rance estuary)
Descent	470m (+325m around Rance estuary)
Time	5hr (+3hr 30min around Rance estuary)
Maps	IGN TOP25 1116ET, 1016ET
Refreshments	Cafés/restaurants in Dinard, Saint-Lunaire, Saint-Briac-sur-Mer, Lancieux
Transport	BreizhGo lines 14, 16; Compagnie Corsaire sea bus (April–October)
Accommodation	Hotels and/or *chambres d'hôtes* in Dinard, Saint-Lunaire, Saint-Briac-sur-Mer, Lancieux; campground in Dinard

The GR34 follows the coast, passing many beautiful beaches. In Dinard, a concrete path snakes around the rocky cliff and tumble of rocks at the water's edge. Later, the GR34 reverts to more natural trails across hillsides. The final 3km of this stage are mostly urban walking.

In **Saint-Malo**, walk south from Porte Saint-Vincent beside the ramparts. Reach the **ferry terminal** (*gare maritime*) on the right after passing a roundabout. Here you have two options.

The official route of the GR34 goes around the Rance estuary: head south from the ramparts, pass the ferry terminal and follow the arc of the Anse des Sablons to reach the **Corniche d'Aleth**. Walk around the Corniche on a pleasant path with views over the estuary, then follow roads and forest trails to the bridge across the river that incorporates a **tidal power station** (*usine marémotrice*). After crossing the bridge, the GR34 follows forest trails to **Dinard** (3hr).

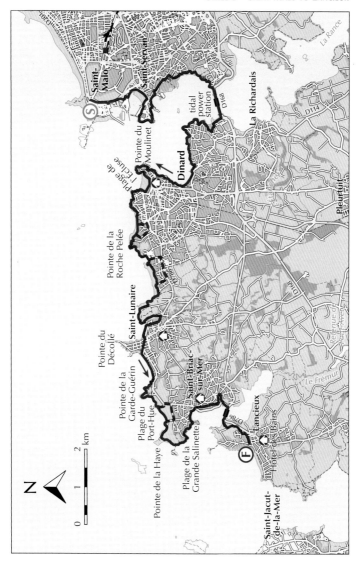

Tour Solidor houses the Cape Horner Museum in Saint-Malo

Sea-bus option

Alternatively, cross the estuary directly from the ferry terminal to Dinard on a 'sea bus' (*bus de mer*). Pick up the GR34 at the Embarcadère on Promenade du Clair de Lune in **Dinard** where the sea bus arrives.

Walk from Dinard's Embarcadère along the embankment and around **Pointe du Moulinet**. At the Pointe, turn right off the main path on a smaller one that descends through rocks close to the water. ◀ The path leads to **Plage de l'Écluse**, passing a large seawater swimming pool (built in 1928). Walk around the beach – pausing, perhaps, at one of the nearby cafés.

Belle Époque villas loom above the opposite shore of the bay.

Two hundred years ago, **Dinard** was a fishing village, overshadowed by the ramparts and forts of its neighbour across the estuary. Then, starting around 1850, the British discovered Dinard. A fashion for seaside holidays blossomed. A Baedeker guidebook published in 1909 described Dinard as 'the leading sea-bathing resort in Brittany owing to its attractive site, its spacious sandy beach, its picturesque views and its pleasant walks. The environs are sprinkled with villas, and it is much frequented by English visitors.' Dinard now stages a British film festival each autumn. The top award is the Hitchcock d'Or.

A statue facing Plage de l'Écluse depicts Alfred Hitchcock confronting two birds – a coy reference to a film that he promoted with a portentous announcement: 'The Birds… is coming.'

Continue on the embankment after the beach to Pointe de la Malouine. A striking sculpture appears to be a large rock lodged incongruously – and precariously! – in the bare branches of a tree. The path leads to **Plage de Saint-Énogat**, a quiet beach. ▶

At the far end of the beach, climb steps carved in steep rock to a path. Turn right here and pass a Thalassa (seawater spa). The path continues along the coast, around **Pointe de Roche Pelée**, and descends to the beach at Port Blanc (café).

Continuing toward Saint-Lunaire, the GR34 goes around a small promontory (marked by a curious half-tower) to reach **Plage de la Fourberie**. Walk along this beach to a large spur of rock that descends to the seashore. Climb up the concrete steps set in this rock to a trail that enters dense vegetation. ▶

This narrow trail continues above the beach and finally descends to a parking area beside the beach. Turn

A high-tide variant (signed and easy to follow) leaves the beach on steps beside a café and rejoins the GR34 beside the Thalassa.

High tide may block access to these steps; a signed variant leaves Port Blanc beach on Rue de la Roche Pelée and rejoins the GR34 at the top of these steps.

Incoming tide at Plage de la Fourberie: it will be necessary to follow the high-tide route above these rocks

left here to follow a trail into the brush and bear right where a path to the left is marked 'Variante Hiver' (winter variant). Turn right at a T-junction on a road that leads to a dirt trail around an estate overlooking Le Nick.

The trail returns to the coast in open country. Walking southeast now, follow the trail to a road. ◄ Turn right here and then right on Boulevard de la Plage, which leads to **Saint-Lunaire**'s Grande Plage (**2h 15min** from Dinard). Walk along the embankment past a massive white building (the former Grand Hotel, built in the 1880s; now converted into apartments) and turn left. At the first intersection, turn right on Boulevard du Général de Gaulle.

Depending on the tide, you can take a short-cut across the small stream here and rejoin the GR34 on the embankment beside Grande Plage.

The GR34 now goes out to **Pointe du Décollé** and back. It's all tarmac, but this headland does have a good view of Cap Fréhel. You can skip Pointe du Décollé by continuing straight on Boulevard du Général de Gaulle to where it intersects the GR34 returning from the Pointe (as shown on the map).

Boulevard du Général de Gaulle leads to Plage de Longchamp. Walk along the embankment beside the beach to a trail that climbs a hill. The trail goes around **Pointe de la Garde-Guérin** (great 360-degree views) and descends to **Plage du Port-Hue**. At the end of this beach, follow a trail beside a *poste de secours* (lifeguard station) up to a broad, sandy track. ◄ The trail goes around a golf course, cuts across the base of **Pointe de la Haye** and passes Île du Perron.

A high-tide variant goes around this beach, following Rue du Port-Hue to rejoin the main route.

Shortly after passing Plage du Perron and an old bunker, turn right on a narrow path. The trail descends to **Plage de la Grande Salinette** in **Saint-Briac-sur-Mer** (**3hr 45min** from Dinard). Turn left beside a *poste de secours*, cut across a narrow promontory past the eye-catching Château de Nessay and follow the arc of Plage de Béchay.

Continue to the end of the embankment beside the beach and walk up steps cut into rock. At the top of these steps, pass a mini-golf, cross a road and continue straight: first on a path across a park, then on Boulevard de la Mer. Where the boulevard ends, turn left on Rue Croix des Marins, a narrow road with attractive old stone houses. Pass the town hall, turn right on Rue de la Haye and right

A beach between Dinard and Saint-Lunaire

on a gravel road. Walk across a footbridge and a broad, grassy area leading to a **bridge over the Frémur estuary**. ▶

After the bridge, walk on a path beside the road. Cross the road where it curves right and follow a path into woods. The path approaches another road: veer right on a gravel road, which becomes a narrow path. At a T-junction, turn left on Rue du Poudouvre. The GR34 crosses Rue de l'Islet and continues straight on Rue Saint-Sieu. To reach the centre of **Lancieux** (where there is a hotel), turn left on Rue de l'Islet and continue on Rue de l'Église.

Crossing this bridge, you enter the Côtes d'Armor Department.

STAGE 6
Lancieux to Saint-Cast-le-Guildo

Start	Lancieux
Finish	Saint-Cast-le-Guildo (Boulevard Surcouf)
Distance	32.5km
Ascent	690m
Descent	710m
Time	8hr
Map	IGN TOP25 1016ET
Refreshments	Cafés/restaurants in Saint-Jacut-de-la-Mer, Le Guildo, Saint-Cast-le-Guildo
Transport	BreizhGo line 14
Accommodation	Hotels and/or *chambres d'hôtes* in Saint-Jacut-de-la-Mer, Saint-Cast-le-Guildo

This stage follows the coast around the bays of Lancieux and Arguenon. You walk along quiet beaches and through marshland. After an inland section that is not so interesting, the trail returns to the coast to go around the Saint Jacut peninsula, passing Pointe du Chevet with its great views over the sea. The route along the western side of the Baie de l'Arguenon is notable for its beaches, starting with one near Le Guildo that offers access at low tide to the curious ringing stones (*pierres sonnantes*) and concluding with Grande Plage in Saint-Cast-le-Guildo.

If you depart from the centre of **Lancieux**, there is no need to walk up Rue de l'Islet to rejoin the GR34; instead, walk northwest on Rue de la Plage to meet the GR34 at the embankment beside the beach. Turn left here and walk along the embankment.

If, on the other hand, you are continuing on the GR34 without a detour into the centre of Lancieux, walk west on Rue Saint-Sieu after crossing Rue de l'Islet. The road curves left to a T-junction: turn right on Rue de la Source, which leads to the embankment.

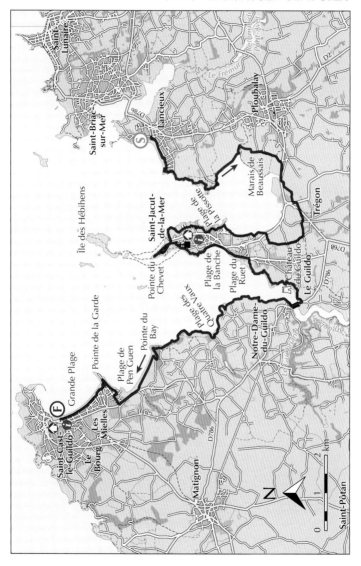

At the end of the embankment, turn left and then right to walk along Boulevard de la Mer. Near the end, the trail branches to the right across a grassy area. Follow a narrow trail above the water to rejoin the road. The trail now heads south beside the coast. Watch for the place where the GR34 turns right to pass through woods. Further on, walk along beaches beside the Baie de Lancieux.

> At low tide there are likely to be people out on the sands, gathering shellfish. This is **pêche à pied** (shore fishing). You will see signs at beaches that specify the sizes and limits of various types of shellfish that can be collected.

About 5km from Lancieux, cross a footbridge over a stream and walk inland through the **Marais (marshland) de Beaussais**, a protected area. Walk generally south across open fields, with occasional trees, on a grass path parallel to a gravel road. The trail approaches a road and curves right to follow a path beside it. Cross the road after 450 metres and continue a short distance in the same direction before crossing a bridge and turning left on a dirt path (**2hr**).

Walking beside majestic oak trees, pass a group of houses enclosed by a stone wall. Turn left on a gravel path away from those houses and left on a road, followed within 75 metres by a right turn on a dirt path. This path continues straight across a road. After 350 metres, turn right and follow a left fork (past a small park) onto Rue du Vieux Bourg.

The road becomes a gravel path through fields. Turn right at an intersection to follow a sign that points to Pointe du Chevet and St Jacut. Walk along this road (which becomes a dirt path) for 1km, then turn right in the forest, where a sign points toward beaches. Cross a road and pick up the trail on the left side of a clearing.

The route now follows the eastern side of the peninsula, passing Plage de la Manchette and its campground. Shortly after **Plage de la Pissote**, turn right at a T-junction, then immediately left. ◄ The GR34 winds its way on

Turn left at this T-junction for direct access to Saint-Jacut-de-la-Mer.

roads and paths through residential areas. After passing the Capitainerie, walk along a narrow coastal trail. Continue past a parking lot to **Pointe du Chevet**, with its fine view of Île des Hébihens.

The GR34 now follows the western side of this peninsula: retrace your steps and, 100 metres after the entrance to the parking lot, turn right on a gravel road. After 200 metres, turn right to pass through a gap in a stone wall and then reverse direction. Walk around a field, with the wall on one side and a wooden fence on the other. The path descends to an embankment beside the sea. Walk on the embankment past the entrance to **Abbaye Saint-Jacut-de-la-Mer**. At the end of the embankment, the GR34 continues up steps to a trail above the beach (**4hr**).

Detour to Saint-Jacut-de-la-Mer
To reach the centre of Saint-Jacut-de-la-Mer from the trail above the beach, turn left on a ramp leading to Rue des Haas. You can return to the GR34 from the centre without backtracking: walk south on Grande Rue past the grocer's and turn right on Rue de l'Arguenon, which reaches the GR34 on the dyke beside the beach.

Follow the trail to a dyke beside **Plage de la Banche**. Walk along the dyke and then a path beside a road. Turn right at a roundabout on Rue du Ruet: a gravel road leads to a small parking area for **Plage du Ruet** and the coastal trail. Walk past an old stone chapel and through a forest to dunes above Plage de Vauver.

After 1km, the trail turns inland beside open fields. The ruins of the **Château du Guildo** loom over the trail. The trail enters the forest, descends to pass below the castle and then climbs to its entrance. ▶

Continue on a trail above the coast and turn right to walk through **Le Guildo** on Rue du Vieux Château, which becomes Chemin des Carmes. Turn right on a road beside a restaurant and cross a **bridge over the Arguenon River**. Descend steps on the right and pass a small park facing the Château du Guildo across the river (**5hr 30min**).

Panels here describe the 'eventful history' of the Château.

Ruins of Château du Guildo

Here you have a choice: the principal route follows Rue des Quais a short distance to Rue des Pierres Sonnantes, where it turns right to enter the forest on a trail. The more interesting option is to walk along the beach with its ringing stones (*pierres sonnantes*) – amphiboles which produce a metallic sound when struck by another stone of the same type. The beach option is only practicable around low tide. (Indeed, a sign with a GR 'X' mark warns of quicksand and the danger of sinking into the mud.) After completing your concert on the stones, continue along the beach to a wooden ramp that enters the forest and rejoins the GR34.

You set off now along the coast toward Saint-Castle-Guildo, 12km away. ◄ It's a pleasant trail through rolling terrain. Occasionally, the trail emerges from the forest to cross open country with views over the Baie de l'Arguenon. Offshore, there are countless rows of *bouchots* (stakes) upon which mussels are cultivated, submerged at high tide and exposed at low tide. **Plage des Quatre Vaux** (3km after the *pierres sonnantes*) is a good place for a break with benches and picnic tables. Behind the beach there is a *crêperie* and a parking area for amphibious vessels used in the cultivation of mussels.

Along this trail there are *bornes de secours* (emergency posts) with numbers that identify their location.

About 2.5km after Plage des Quatre Vaux, the GR34 curves around **Pointe du Bay**. Vast beaches leading to Saint-Cast-le-Guildo lie ahead. The GR34 descends to the first of these, **Plage de Pen Guen**. Near the end of this beautiful beach, turn left beside a restaurant, walk through a parking lot and uphill beside a road. Turn right at a roundabout and walk through a residential area toward **Pointe de la Garde**.

Upon reaching the Oratory of Notre Dame de la Garde, the GR34 doubles back to the left on a trail that leads to Boulevard de la Garde. Right turns on Rue des 2 Rives and Rue Corniche de la Plage lead to **Grande Plage**. Follow the pavement beside this beach to a roundabout that gives access to the centre of **Saint-Cast-le-Guildo** on Boulevard Surcouf.

An amphibious mussel field tender

STAGE 7

*Saint-Cast-le-Guildo to
Petit Trécelin*

Start	Saint-Cast-le-Guildo
Finish	Petit Trécelin
Distance	17.5km
Ascent	585m
Descent	485m
Time	4hr 30min
Map	IGN TOP25 1016ET
Refreshments	Café/restaurants in Port-à-la-Duc, Petit Trécelin
Transport	BreizhGo line 14
Accommodation	Hotel in Petit Trécelin

The leading feature of this stage is a long walk along the Baie de la Fresnaye, with its succession of small beaches. If the tide is low, you can marvel at the countless rows of *bouchots* in the bay, where mussels grow. That sight – and this walk along the GR34 – may whet your appetite for a dinner of *moules marinières*, accompanied by *frites* and a good white wine!

The Sémaphore – a large, white building bristling with electronic gear on its roof – is part of the network of stations that regulate maritime traffic in the Channel and respond to emergencies.

This stage begins at the roundabout in **Saint-Cast-le-Guildo** where Boulevard Surcouf meets Boulevard de la Mer. Walk north along Boulevard de la Mer and, where that road begins to climb, continue on Promenade du Soleil Levant. Yachts and fishing vessels fill the harbour; cafés and restaurants line the road.

At the end of the harbour, pass a memorial to 'Marins-Pêcheurs disparus en Mer' (fishermen lost at sea) and walk beside Rue du Sémaphore up to **Pointe de l'Isle**. ◀ At the top of this hill there is a memorial to those who escaped from France to continue the fight against Germany during World War II and a cannon that saw action in the Battle of Saint-Cast.

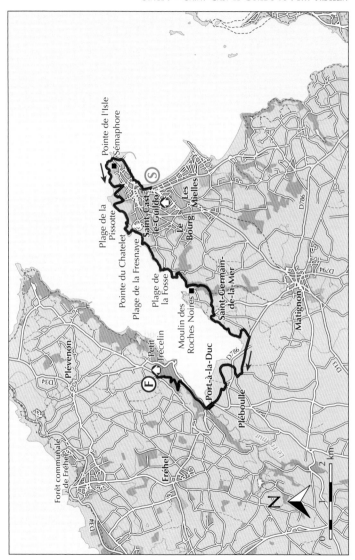

THE BATTLE OF SAINT-CAST

The Battle of Saint-Cast was a minor skirmish in the Seven Years War, but a glorious Breton victory in local memory. In September 1758, British war-ships landed soldiers at Saint-Lunaire with plans to cross the Rance and attack Saint-Malo. Bad weather compelled the ships to withdraw, and the attack was abandoned. The soldiers marched overland to Saint-Cast, the nearest landing place sheltered from a westerly gale, to be re-embarked aboard the ships. French soldiers, commanded by the Duke d'Aiguillon, and Breton militia led by local nobles pursued the British and attacked them on the beach below Saint-Cast. D'Aiguillon's command post was a windmill on a hill overlooking the beach. The British lost 800 men – mostly prisoners – in making their escape.

D'Aiguillon, as the governor of Brittany, was involved around this time in a running conflict with Breton aristocrats who resisted royal encroach-ments upon their privileges. A leading figure among the Bretons defying the Crown was La Chalotais, *procureur-général* (public prosecutor) of the Breton *parlement* (appellate court). D'Aiguillon's opponents were keen to belittle his role in the Battle of Saint-Cast. Playing upon d'Aiguillon's reputation as a womaniser, La Chalotais insinuated that he had shown more interest in the miller's wife (*la meunière*) than the battle: *'le duc d'Aiguillon s'est plus couvert de farine que de gloire'* ('the duke d'Aiguillon covered himself more in flour than in glory'). The comment may be apocryphal, but it gave a name to a café/pastry shop in Saint-Cast: la Belle Meunière.

Laplace, anchored to shelter from a storm in 1950, detonated a World War II magnetic mine. The ship sank; 51 of the its 92 crew died in this tragedy.

Turn left to walk along the coastal trail above cliffs. Fort La Latte and Cap Fréhel – highlights of the next stage – are visible across the Baie de la Fresnaye. Pass a sombre memorial to the frigate *Laplace* and walk inland around a campground. ◀ The GR34 follows several roads (well signed) that lead back to the coast above **Plage de la Pissotte**. Walking around **Pointe du Chatelet** you have a good view over the bay, with rows of mussel *bouchots* (**1hr 15min**).

The trail down to **Plage de la Fresnaye** is rocky and requires care. Once it reaches the bottom, the trail turns left and goes right back up. Continuing along the coastal trail, walk past a campground and descend to a boat ramp at **Plage de la Fosse**. Further on, pass through a

parking area for amphibious vehicles used in the cultivation of mussels.

Follow a smooth path through a forest. ▶ Continue straight to the picturesque ruins of the Moulin de la Mer (**2hr 15min**). The GR34 turns right here, crosses a stream on a footbridge and follows a trail to the right signposted for Pointe St Efficace. However, the trail around Pointe St Efficace is not very interesting, as dense vegetation blocks the view. Therefore, the route proposed here goes directly to the west side of this peninsula via Saint-Germain-de-la-Mer: go straight up the trail after crossing the footbridge beside the Moulin de la Mer and continue to **Saint-Germain-de-la-Mer**. Walk to the left of the chapel in this village, then turn right where a sign points to 'Lavoir Source – 300m'. Follow the trail to its intersection with the GR34 and turn left.

The trail continues along the coast for a kilometre and then turns inland (left). Turn right on a residential road opposite a magnificent stone building with sky-blue windows, then right on a road that leads to a main road with fast traffic. Turn right again and walk 400 metres beside this road.

An impressive stone building beside a small *ria* – Moulin des Roches Noires, formerly a tidal mill – stands on the opposite shore.

Ruins of the Moulin de la Mer

Continue straight on a trail into the woods where the road curves right. Walk through a group of farm buildings, workshops and homes. Turn right at a T-junction, cross a stream and turn right at another T-junction. Cross the road and continue straight on a small road across open fields toward Pointe de Crissouët. A discreet GR mark at a T-junction indicates a left turn: follow the road to the left to reach the main road at **Port-à-la-Duc** beside the Frémur River, where there are picnic tables (**4hr**).

Cross a **bridge** and turn right, then veer left on a trail above the road. The trail curves to the left after about 1km and then turns sharply right after 300 metres on a trail that descends in the woods, with GR marks showing the way. The trail reaches **Petit Trécelin**, where there is a pleasant hotel/restaurant.

STAGE 8
Petit Trécelin to Sables-d'Or-les-Pins

Start	Petit Trécelin
Finish	Sables-d'Or-les-Pins (centre)
Distance	22km
Ascent	825m
Descent	875m
Time	6hr
Map	IGN TOP25 1016ET
Refreshments	Café/restaurants at Cap Fréhel, Pléhérel-Plage, Sables-d'Or-les-Pins
Transport	BreizhGo line 2
Accommodation	A *chambres d'hôtes* in Plévenon (700 metres from Fort La Latte); hotel in Pléhérel-Plage; hotels, *chambres d'hôtes*, campground in Sables-d'Or-les-Pins

The highlight of this stage is a site that receives Michelin's three-star rating: Cap Fréhel. You will enjoy the walk from Fort La Latte to the Cap, crossing heathland beside cliffs that stand 70m above the sea, with the tall lighthouse piercing the horizon. The trail from Cap Fréhel along the coast to Sables-d'Or-les-Pins is less dramatic but still beautiful as you pass a succession of broad, sandy beaches.

A sign beside the road near the hotel in **Petit Trécelin** points to the GR34. Follow the trail to a road. Turn left, walk 100 metres beside the road and turn right up wooden steps into the forest. The trail follows the coast, with open country (offering views over the Baie de la Fresnaye) interspersed with forest. The trail descends on steps through a hairpin right turn, turns right at a T-junction and continues to a beach. Turn left and walk a short distance on the beach before turning left again where a sign points to Port Saint-Géran to climb back into the forest.

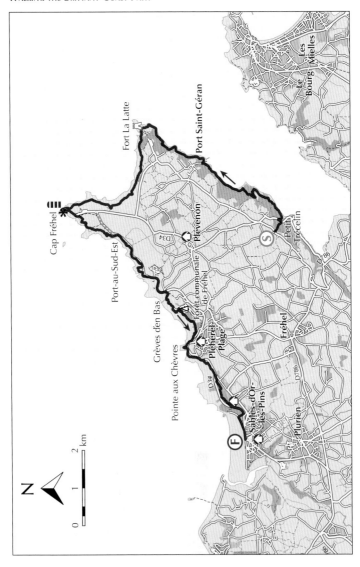

The trail from here is quite hilly. After one extended climb, it descends to **Port Saint-Géran**. A sign points to Fort La Latte and Cap Fréhel; turn left into a parking area and then right on a trail. Follow the trail through woods and open terrain above the coast. Soon, **Fort La Latte** appears dramatically (**2hr 15min**).

> **Fort La Latte** occupies a strong defensive position on a rocky spur 60m above the water. The fort was besieged and captured in 1379 by du Guesclin, a famous Breton knight who served the French crown, but it successfully resisted an English siege in 1490. It is open now for visits. Fort La Latte has featured in numerous films, notably *The Vikings* (1958). Of course, its appearance in that film was anachronistic: there were no castles like this in Western Europe during the Vikings' heyday in the 9th–10th centuries.

After Fort La Latte, the GR34 passes through a pine forest and enters a vast heathland, with gorse and heather growing in profusion. There are awesome views over

Fort La Latte

Cap Fréhel

pink sandstone cliffs. This is a fragile, protected area, so it is important to stay on the trails that lead to **Cap Fréhel** (**3hr 15min**).

Cap Fréhel is one of Brittany's greatest headlands – and an important bird sanctuary with its offshore rock, the Fauconnière. Two lighthouses stand here. The smaller structure, Tour Vauban, was built in 1702; it operated with coal, fish oil and finally vegetable oil. The tall one, reaching 103m above the sea, was built in 1950 (replacing a lighthouse built in 1847 and destroyed in 1944); its light carries as far as 120km in clear weather.

Leaving Cap Fréhel, pick up the trail beside Tour Vauban. The GR34 turns southwest to follow the coast. You pass **Port-au-Sud-Est** – a beautiful, broad beach. The trail winds its way through the heath, occasionally shifting to a bicycle path beside a road. Along the way, there are great views over cliffs and beaches (La Fosse and Grèves d'en Bas). ◀

Side-trails lead to these beaches.

Layers of sedimentary sandstone offer lessons in geology along the way.

Eventually, the GR34 itself descends to **Grèves d'en Bas** on a trail over a hill that may be overgrown with vegetation. After a short walk along the beach, enter a **campground**. Walk through the campground (generally southwest, with occasional GR marks) for nearly 1km to a parking lot. Walk up a road to the right that intersects a main road. ▶ The beach below is the Anse du Croc; in the distance Cap Fréhel and its lighthouse are visible (**5hr**).

Turn left here for the centre of Plérérel-Plage.

Turn right on the coastal trail (direction: Cap d'Erquy). It approaches **Pointe aux Chèvres**, then turns sharply left. The trail reaches a road, which it follows for 150 metres before turning right into a forest. At places where the route emerges from the forest, the land is carpeted with bright yellow gorse in the spring, joined by purple heather in the summer and interspersed with pine and oak trees.

The trail – broad, smooth and well marked – crosses the road and continues in the forest. At the next intersection with the road, turn left to walk beside it, passing a large hotel and pond on the left; then turn right on a trail into woods between two large stones.

The trail leads to a beach: turn left on Promenade Émile Barrier and continue on Boulevard de la Mer into **Sables-d'Or-les-Pins**. Turn left on Allée des Acacias for the centre.

Sables-d'Or-les-Pins was founded in 1922–24 by a promoter who had big plans for a luxurious resort that would rival those in Normandy, such as Deauville. He went bankrupt in the 1930s, and the town never lived up to his dreams.

STAGE 9
Sables-d'Or-les-Pins to Pléneuf-Val-André

Start	Sables-d'Or-les-Pins (centre)
Finish	Pléneuf-Val-André (Promenade de la Digue)
Distance	21km
Ascent	660m
Descent	655m
Time	5hr 15min
Map	IGN TOP25 0916ET
Refreshments	Cafés/restaurants at Pointe du Champ du Port, Erquy, Pléneuf-Val-André
Transport	BreizhGo line 2
Accommodation	Hotels, *chambres d'hôtes* in Erquy, Pléneuf-Val-André

The theme for this stage is… beaches! They spread broadly before towns with refreshments and accommodation – Sables-d'Or-les-Pins and Pléneuf-Val-André at the two ends of the stage, as well as Erquy along the way – and they lie in remote areas along the route. In all, a dozen beaches with names, not to mention other patches of sand and rock below hills and cliffs.

From **Sables-d'Or-les-Pins**, the GR34 continues west on Boulevard de la Mer from its intersection with Allée des Acacias. At the end of the boulevard, turn left on a sandy trail that goes around the northeast side of a tidal estuary and continue on a road – Promenade du Lac – back to Allée des Acacias. (You could, of course, simply walk up Allée des Acacias to its intersection with Promenade du Lac.) Turn right to walk southwest on a bicycle path beside Allée des Acacias. After 250 metres the GR34 turns right and continues around the estuary, curving left.

Signs beside the bridges describe their construction and original use for a railway in service from 1924 to 1948.

The trail soon reaches a road, curves right past a campground (**Les Salines**) and crosses marshland (*marais*) on two old, restored bridges: Pont des Marais and Passerelle de la Cotière. ◄ The walk across these bridges

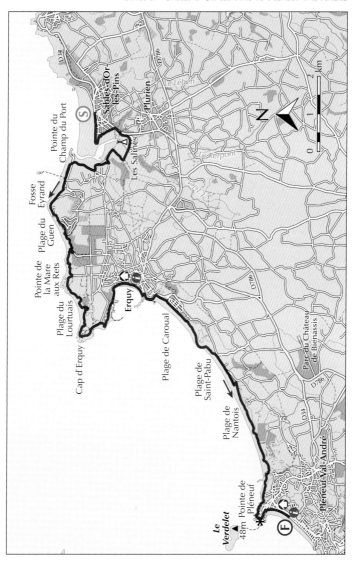

offers a pleasant perspective over the marshland and meandering **Islet River**.

After crossing the second bridge, turn right and descend on a path through a forest to a road. Turn left at a T-junction with Rue de la Vallée Denis and follow the GR34 as it branches left off that road on a trail that climbs across open ground to a sharp right turn and descends back to the road. Follow the road to the left.

Turn right at a T-junction and walk to a parking area for a beach (**1hr**). Turn left on a trail beside the beach, passing enormous rocks between the beach and the road. The route curves left around **Fosse Eyrand** and passes a large holiday centre. The GR34 climbs a hill to the left here and follows a well-signed route above the beach, **Plage du Guen**, through a residential area. This route may be necessary at high tide, but a beach walk is preferable if the tide permits: just after the holiday centre, follow a concrete path to the right, which leads to the beach. Enjoy a 1km walk along this beach and then leave it on a paved path to rejoin the high-tide route of the GR34. Turn right on a trail that climbs into a pine forest (**1hr 45min**).

The GR34 continues from here along the coast, offering breathtaking views of beautiful beaches. The sea sparkles emerald on a sunny day. About 500 metres from Plage du Guen, descend toward Plage du Portuais

Plage du Lourtuais

Les Châtelets
(Cap d'Erquy)

and then climb back to the ridge on wooden steps. After rounding rocky **Pointe de la Mare aux Rets**, descend steps to a trail just above **Plage de Lourtuais**, walk a short distance on the level trail and climb back up another set of steps to a gravel path. Turn right at a signpost to continue on the coastal trail.

Walk around **Cap d'Erquy** on a rocky trail. Pass a parking area and continue southeast on a gravel path beside a road to a *corps de garde* and, on a spur of rock below it, a *four à boulets*.

> A **four à boulets** – shot oven – was used in the days of wooden sailing ships to heat shot that would be fired at enemy ships. The procedure for heating the shot, loading it into the muzzle of a cannon and firing the cannon was difficult and dangerous, but if red-hot shot struck a ship, that ship was probably doomed. Shot ovens lost their utility in the 19th century, but heated shot left a mark in the French language: *tirer à boulets rouges* means to criticise harshly.

Walk down to the *four à boulets* and continue past old quarries on the trail to **Erquy**. The trail concludes on wooden steps down to Rue du Port beside Erquy's commercial fishing port (**2hr 45min**). Restaurants along this road face moorings for recreational boats. Follow the pavement curving to the right between Boulevard de la Mer and the beach.

SCALLOPS

Erquy is one of the leading ports for landing *coquilles Saint-Jacques* (scallops) in Brittany. The 'Coquille Saint-Jacques des Côtes-d'Armor', a Protected Geographic Indication within the European Union, accounts for 90% of Breton production and nearly 50% of French production of this shellfish. The fishing of scallops in the Baie de Saint-Brieuc is strictly regulated in order to maintain stocks: the season runs from late October to late April (thereby leaving the scallops undisturbed during their reproduction period). Boats using dragnets rake the seabed and collect scallops for a maximum of 45 minutes per day, 2 days per week. The annual Fête de la Coquille Saint-Jacques takes place in April, rotating among Erquy, Saint-Quay-Portrieux and Paimpol.

Walk along the pavement, passing a row of flagpoles with flags of EU countries. At the end of the pavement, walk up a road and make a hairpin left turn on a gravel path. Turn right at a T-junction and walk beside Rue de la Corniche. Turn right on Rue des Sternes and descend to **Plage de Caroual**.

Walk on the pavement above this beach and along Promenade de la Mer, passing apartment buildings with distinctive balcony ornamentation suggesting ocean waves, and continue straight on a narrow trail beside the beach. Turn left at a boat ramp and immediately right on a trail. A further 200 metres along the trail, where a side-trail branches right to the beach, the GR34 climbs and emerges in open country above the sea.

The route from here to Pointe de Pléneuf follows the coast, passing a succession of beaches backed by rocky cliffs and spurs. The trail descends to **Plage de Saint-Pabu** about 3.5km from Erquy and continues on a road beside the beach. Where the road diverges from the beach, the GR34 continues straight for 500 metres and turns left away from the beach to traverse a higher slope. The trail

*Approaching
Pléneuf-Val-André
in the evening*

descends to **Plage de Nantois**, where you walk on rocks for 200 metres (or, more comfortably, on the beach at low tide) before continuing on a grass trail (**4hr 30min**).

Follow the GR34 on a path past a golf course and the ruins of a stone house. The trail climbs and plunges into a hilly area of bushes and ferns before descending to another vast beach, Plage des Vallées. Cross a parking area and walk up steps where a sign points to Port Val André and Port Dahouët. The trail now curves around **Pointe de Pléneuf**, with great views and benches for pausing to appreciate them. ▶

The island offshore, Verdelet, is a bird sanctuary.

Descend to Pléneuf-Val-André on Rue de la Corniche, which becomes Rue du Coteau. Turn right on Rue de la Tour d'Auvergne, which winds down to the town's beach. Turn left to walk along Quai Célestin Bouglé and then Promenade de la Digue. Rue Winston Churchill beside the casino leads to the centre of **Pléneuf-Val-André**.

STAGE 10
Pléneuf-Val-André to Hillion

Start	Pléneuf-Val-André
Finish	Hillion (centre)
Distance	26.5km
Ascent	930m
Descent	930m
Time	6hr 45min
Map	IGN TOP25 0916ET
Refreshments	Cafés/restaurants in Dahouët, Jospinet, Hillion
Transport	BreizhGo line 2
Accommodation	*Chambres d'hôtes* in Dahouët, Morieux (1km); hotel in Hillion

This stage offers many kilometres of agreeable coastal walking: the trail drops occasionally to beaches that lie along the route, but generally remains on higher ground, offering good views over the coast and the sea. The stage also includes something completely different: a rugged trail that follows one side of the Gouessant estuary inland through forest to a bridge and returns to the coast on the other side.

This stage begins in **Pléneuf-Val-André** on Promenade de la Digue opposite the casino and continues along the Promenade. Near the end of the pavement, just after passing a sailing centre, turn left on Rue des Sablons, which curves right and becomes a dirt path that climbs and offers a final view over Pléneuf-Val-André and its enormous beach. The trail now follows the coast, going around two headlands – Guette and **Grande Guette** – enclosing a small beach, Anse du Pissot.

An 18th-century **corps de garde** stands on the latter headland. According to an explanatory plaque, it protected the area against English and Dutch

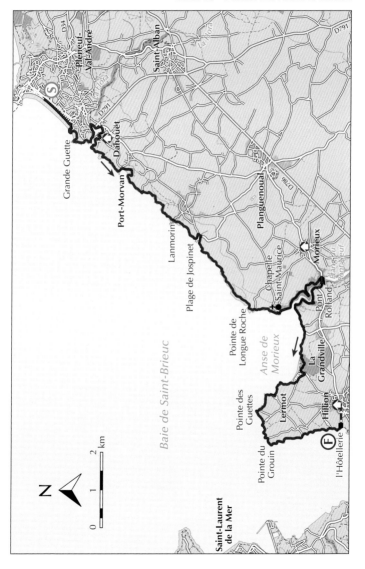

warships. The two cannons mounted below it went into action many times – *'souvent avec succès'* ('often with success'). The gunners presumably appreciated their magnificent view over the Baie de Saint-Brieuc.

The GR34 reaches a channel leading from the sea to **Dahouët**. Pass an oratory above the channel and descend stone steps to a harbour filled with pleasure craft. Walk along Quai des Terre-Neuvas (passing restaurants) and cross a bridge to the right. Go around the harbour and turn left on Quai du Mûrier, which climbs from the harbour, and left on Chemin de la Sancie. Turn right after 100 metres on a gravel road and right again after another 100 metres on a dirt path. This path follows the coast and leaves the residential area.

Turn right in front of a stone building where a sign points to Port-Morvan. Walk to a beach and turn left on a trail that follows the coast. The bay fills the horizon, with a bucolic scene of rolling countryside inland. The trail descends to **Port-Morvan**, a village with a small beach (**1h 45min**).

Lighthouse (Phare de la Petite Muette) at the entrance to Dahouët harbour

Walk up a road at the entrance to the beach and turn right on Rue de la Fontenelle. After 250 metres, turn right on a trail into fields, following the contours of hills along the coast. Descend to a beach (Grève du Vaughlin), pass a parking area and climb again. As you walk, the trail ahead is visible, snaking through vegetation on the slopes. At **Lanmorin**, panels describe *pêche à pied* (shore fishing) and *mytiliculture* (mussel cultivation).

Port-Morvan

MUSSELS

The bays of Saint-Brieuc and Mont-Saint-Michel are Brittany's leading areas for the cultivation of *moules* (mussels). It's a complicated process: mature mussels release larvae in the spring. These larvae drift in the water and attach themselves to cords that have been strung between posts. The larvae grow and become *naissains* (spat). (For mussels cultivated in the Baie de Saint-Brieuc, this stage takes place on the Atlantic coast.) Cords covered with juvenile mussels are wound around *bouchots* (stakes) implanted in the seabed, where the mussels grow for 12–18 months to a size large enough to be harvested. You will see flat-bottomed amphibious boats that tend and harvest the mussels.

Just over a kilometre from Lanmorin, the trail descends to **Plage de Jospinet**, where there is a restaurant (**2hr 45min**). Cross a bridge and turn right on a trail that climbs. The trail is smooth and easy as it goes up and

89

down through vegetation (gorse, ferns) and across open fields.

Coming around **Pointe de Longue Roche**, there are views over the broad Anse de Morieux. Descend to a parking area above Plage de Béliard and continue straight along a trail. Pass **Chapelle Saint-Maurice** on its spur of land and a parking area above Plage Saint-Maurice.

Turn left on the road here to reach Morieux (1km), where there is accommodation.

Here, the GR34 leaves the coast and follows a trail up the Gouessant River. It climbs quite steeply in places and then descends in dense forest to a bridge, **Pont Rolland** (**4hr 30min**). ◄ The majestic stone building with arched windows and a turret on the opposite shore was a hydroelectric power station (1935–2013).

Cross the bridge to follow the GR34 back to the coast on the left bank of the river. Shortly after the bridge, climb steps on the left and turn right on a level trail. Cross the road coming from the bridge and continue north on the same trail. The trail curves left, crosses a tributary stream on a footbridge and turns right to go uphill. The winding river is visible below the trail, and soon Chapelle Saint-Maurice comes into view across the estuary.

The GR34 now follows the coast generally westward on a pleasant, easy trail. Upon reaching a road, with Plage de Bon Abri on the right, turn left and walk 100 metres, then turn right beside a mussel facility. Continue 300 metres on this road and turn right on a trail that returns to the coast.

Walk through the parking area for Plage de Lermot and follow a road to the right. Continue straight when the road makes a hairpin left turn and walk on a trail toward **Pointe des Guettes**. When you walk around this headland, the Baie de Saint-Brieuc opens before you. Signs now point to Pointe du Grouin (**6hr**).

Hillion's Maison de la Baie has informative exhibits about local geography and wildlife – in particular, birds.

The trail turns left at **Pointe du Grouin** and follows the coast south. Along the way, pass the ruins of a small *abri des douaniers* (customs officers' shelter). A side-trail on the left, 1km after that structure, leads to the Maison de la Baie. ◄ The trail arrives at a place called **l'Hôtellerie**. The GR34 continues along the coast, but turn left here on a tarmac road for **Hillion** (500 metres).

STAGE 11

Hillion to Saint-Laurent-de-la-Mer

Start	Hillion
Finish	Saint-Laurent-de-la-Mer (centre)
Distance	17km
Ascent	275m
Descent	230m
Time	4hr
Map	IGN TOP25 0916OT
Refreshments	Cafés/restaurants in Yffiniac, Langueux, Port du Légué, Saint-Brieuc, Saint-Laurent-de-la-Mer
Transport	BreizhGo line 2; TUB lines 20, D; railway service at Saint-Brieuc
Accommodation	Hotels and/or *chambres d'hôtes* in Saint-Brieuc, Saint-Laurent-de-la-Mer

This stage goes around the inner part of the Baie de Saint-Breuc, the Anse d'Yffiniac, and passes near Saint-Brieuc, a major city. The route stays close to sea level and goes through urban areas, so the countryside and the sea views are not as memorable as elsewhere along the GR34. If the time available for your trek is limited, you could shorten this stage by taking a bus from Hillion to Saint-Brieuc and/or another from Saint-Brieuc to Saint-Laurent-de-la-Mer.

Walk west from **Hillion** on Rue de l'Hôtellerie to rejoin the GR34. Turn left and follow the trail along the coast in and out of woods, mostly close to sea level. After 1.3km, walk into open country on a gravel road. Plaques embedded in the road at 100-metre intervals give distances up to and down from 1500. Just after the second 1300-metre mark, turn right to follow a trail upon a dyke.

Turn right on a road after 600 metres to cross a bridge, then right on a dyke that curves in an arc back to the same road. Turn right to cross another bridge and walk carefully beside a road that lacks a good verge for

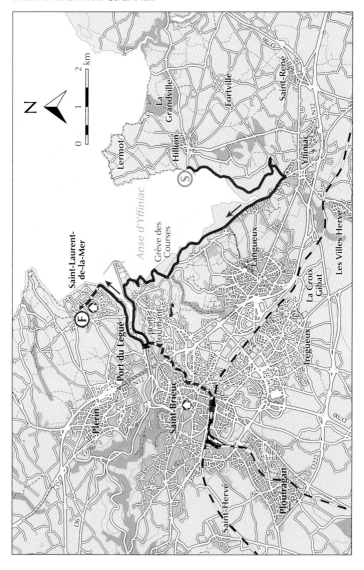

pedestrians. Finally, after nearly 500 metres beside this road, turn right at a T-junction on a road that has a good walking path beside it.

The GR34 follows this path for 4km, mostly close to the **Anse d'Yffiniac**. It passes a *crêperie* in **Langueux** and continues straight where the road turns left. Walk through a forest and turn right at a T-junction on Chemin des Nouetttes. ▶

> You pass the **Grève des Courses** beach, which gained its name from the horse races that were staged here under the authority of a decree issued by Napoleon, promoting equine husbandry to supply his armies.

Turn right at an intersection and walk past an animal shelter to the coast. ▶ Turn left to walk on a trail parallel to the coast. Turn left again on a road, then immediately right; continue straight on Rue Estienne d'Orves through a residential area. Turn right after 200 metres on a narrow road that slips between houses. At the bottom of this road, turn left on a trail that curves above the coastal rocks.

Descend steps to a path leading to **Plage du Valais**. Walk up a road (away from the beach), make a hairpin right turn on a dirt road and bear right when that road forks. Follow a trail to the right when the road curves sharply left and walk in front of cabins perched over the Anse d'Yffiniac (**2hr 30min**).

After the cabins, walk through high grass above a warehouse on the right. The trail traverses high ground, descends steeply in the woods and reaches steps that descend to a road beside the river (Le Gouët). This is **Port du Légué**, Saint-Brieuc's harbour. ▶ Turn left on the road and walk past a lock, shipyards, warehouses – and a well-situated café. Turn right at a roundabout onto Quai Armez and then immediately right to cross the river on a swing bridge (**pont tournant, 3h 45min**) If that bridge is open for boat traffic, you can cross the river on the **Pont de Pierre** 850 metres upstream.

Along this route, the Briqueterie museum presents the industrial history of the area (including the train that ran along the route followed by the GR34).

A bilingual sign indicates the city limit of Saint-Brieuc/ Sant Brieg.

Looming above you are the ruins of Tour de Cesson, the donjon of a 14th-century castle.

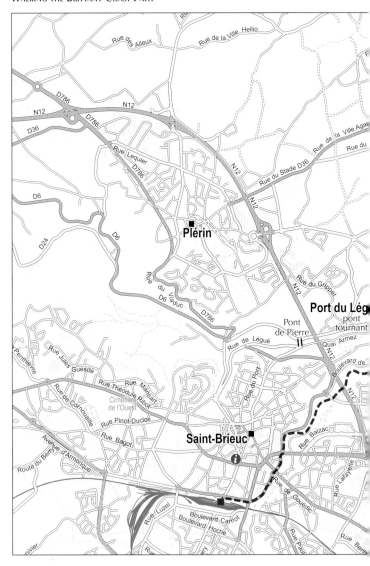

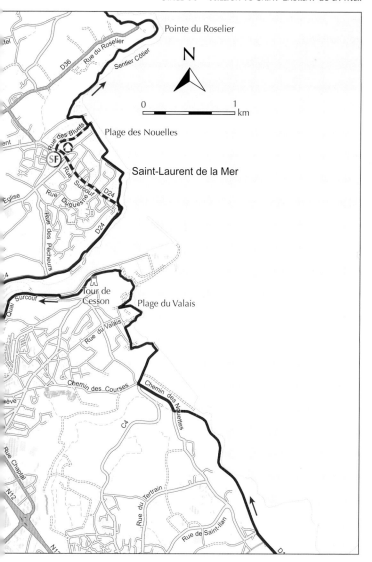

Port du Légué below Saint-Brieuc

Saint-Brieuc is named after the Welsh monk Brioc, a Founder Saint who established an oratory here in the sixth century. It is a major city with all facilities. Turn left at the roundabout on Boulevard de la Mer to reach the city centre; the city map shows the route from here to the railway station (3km). The first part of the route is a path through woods, with a few signposts indicating the way. Eventually, a path leads up to a street beside a roundabout. Follow Boulevard Waldeck-Rousseau south from the roundabout, and continue on Boulevard Charner to the railway station. You will not be alone (or bored) if you visit Saint-Brieuc during the Pentecost weekend, when the Art Rock festival takes place, featuring music, theatre, dance, street art, gastronomy…

Turn right after crossing the river and walk beside the road (D24), passing Rue du Phare on the right. Then, 2km after the swing bridge, the GR34 branches right off Rue de la Mer. To reach the centre of **Saint-Laurent-de-la-Mer**, leave the GR34 here and continue uphill on Rue de la Mer, which becomes Rue Surcouf. To continue north on the GR34 without visiting the town centre, refer to the description in Stage 12.

STAGE 12

Saint-Laurent-de-la-Mer to Saint-Quay-Portrieux

Start	Saint-Laurent-de-la-Mer (centre)
Finish	Saint-Quay-Portrieux (Boulevard du Général de Gaulle)
Distance	26km
Ascent	980m
Descent	1005m
Time	7hr
Map	IGN TOP25 0916OT
Refreshments	Cafés/restaurants at Martin-Plage, Les Rosaires, Binic, Plage des Godelins, Étables-sur-Mer, Plage du Moulin, Saint-Quay-Portrieux
Transport	BreizhGo line 1
Accommodation	Hotels and/or *chambres d'hôtes* in Binic, Étables-sur-Mer, Saint-Quay-Portrieux

This stage is a majestic parade of beaches: some are long and broad (in particular, those around Binic and Saint-Quay-Portrieux); others are narrowly enclosed by cliffs. The GR34 follows a pleasant coastal path with views over the Baie de Saint-Brieuc.

If you're departing from the centre of **Saint-Laurent-de-la-Mer**, near the post office, you can rejoin the GR34 by walking northeast on Rue des Bleuets: turn left after 500 metres onto Chemin Saint-Jean.

If you did not leave the GR34 at the end of Stage 11, the route branches right off the main road below Saint-Laurent-de-la-Mer at 2, Rue de la Mer – a driveway, in fact, that leads to a narrow path above the bay. Turn left on Rue des Trois Plages and then right at a T-junction with a road that leads to **Plage des Nouelles**. Turn left to walk along the embankment beside this beach. At the end of the embankment, turn left and then immediately right on Chemin Saint-Jean (meeting here the route from the centre of Saint-Laurent-de-la-Mer described above).

Walk on Chemin Saint-Jean and turn left at a T-junction with Rue du Dr Violette. Pass a group of white buildings (Centre Hélio-Marin, which provides special education for handicapped children) and turn right on a trail into the woods. Walk through the woods and continue on a tarmac road overlooking the bay. Fork right on a narrow path along the coast to reach **Pointe du Roselier**.

Pointe du Roselier is a good place to pause: there is a *four à boulets* with a detailed explanation of how it was used. On higher ground, there is a group of monuments within a semi-circle of trees open to the bay. The principal monument is dedicated to those who perished at sea (*Aux péris en mer*). Other monuments commemorate specific shipwrecks and losses of life. Large slabs of stone offer places to sit where you can admire the view and reflect upon the perils faced by those who go down to the sea in ships...

Monument at Pointe du Roselier to those who perished at sea

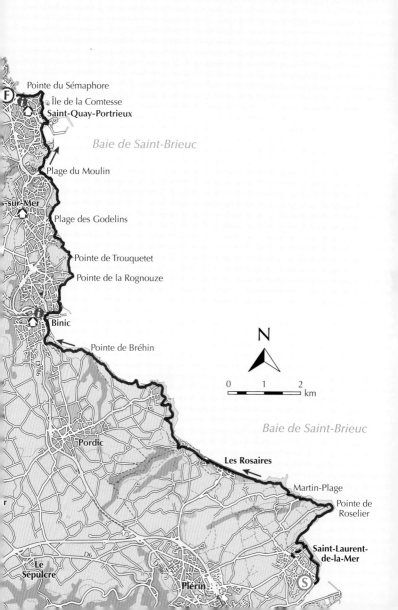

Pointe du Sémaphore

Île de la Comtesse

Saint-Quay-Portrieux

Baie de Saint-Brieuc

Plage du Moulin

-sur-Mer

Plage des Godelins

Pointe de Trouquetet

Pointe de la Rognouze

Binic

Pointe de Bréhin

N

0   1   2
km

Pordic

Baie de Saint-Brieuc

Les Rosaires

Martin-Plage

Pointe de Roselier

Saint-Laurent-de-la-Mer

Le Sépulcre

Plérin

The trail descends to **Martin-Plage**. Turn left and walk up Rue de Port-Martin, fork right and turn right on Allée de Port-Martin. Soon, a left turn returns to a beautiful coastal trail above the water that leads to Plage des Rosaires (**1hr 30min**). Turn left here to walk on the beach itself or a trail beside it – but not on the long mound of stones (*galets*): a sign explains the fragility of these stones and the importance of protecting them.

Continue on an embankment and, where it narrows, turn left into **Les Rosaires** on Rue du Poher, right on Avenue du Tregor and fork right on Rue des Horizons. Continue straight on a trail and turn right at a T-junction. After passing a parking area, turn right on a path that climbs gently and fork left on a broad trail that enters a forest.

The trail moves inland along the edge of a field. Turn right at the intersection of two roads, walk over the crest of a small hill – and the sea fills the horizon. Follow the road down and continue on a trail, which soon meets another road. Turn right toward the coast on this road, which again leads to a trail. As you walk along this trail, Binic comes into view.

The trail descends and approaches a beach (Petit Havre), but climbs back up before reaching it. After entering open country on a ridge opposite Binic, descend a rocky slope to **Pointe de Bréhin** and beyond. A sign at the bottom points to Binic. Cross a ravine and climb the opposite slope. The trail goes up and down through a forest and passes the Camp des Bernains – a site of settlements dating back to Neolithic times – where the network of trails around the site complicates the task of following the GR34. Carry on generally northwest.

When you emerge from the wooded area, walk downhill southwest across an open field to a surfaced road. Follow that road a short distance northwest into a forest and continue right on a trail where the road curves left. The GR34 enters **Binic** on a road in a residential area (**4hr 15min**). Walk along an embankment between Plage de la Banche and a *pétanque* ground. Cross a footbridge and turn right to walk along quays that are lined with restaurants, hotels and shops. ◄

Binic's annual Folks [sic] Blues Festival attracts big crowds during a weekend in July.

Continue past the Bureau du Port and curve left on Quai Surcouf. Upon reaching the breakwater, turn left to walk up a zig-zag ramp to a path between homes and a steep slope down to a beach. A broad trail follows the coast, passing **Pointe de la Rognouze** and **Pointe de Trouquetet**. This trail ends 3km from Binic with a long set of steps, followed by a narrow path hemmed in by fences.

At the exit from the narrow path, turn right on a road at a T-junction. The road leads to steps down to a trail above **Plage des Godelins (5h 30min)**. Descend to the beach (restaurant). ▶ Turn left to walk on Boulevard Legris, then bear right and resume walking on the coastal trail. The trail goes up and down moderately for 1.5km and descends to **Plage du Moulin** (restaurant). Walk past the entrance to the beach and continue on a quiet road that climbs and descends, passing a park with picnic tables and a good view over the sea.

A road runs inland from here to Étables-sur-Mer (1km).

The GR34 now reaches Saint-Quay-Portrieux. A path branches right off the road and descends a short distance to Rue du Port És Leu. Turn right and then immediately left to walk along Quai Robert Richet beside the harbour. Curve right on Quai de la République and, near the end of this road, turn left and walk up steps to a path above Plage de Comtesse. Close offshore is the **Île de la Comtesse**.

The path – the 'Chemin de Ronde' – continues around **Pointe du Sémaphore**. The commercial centre of

Saint-Quay's seawater swimming pool at low tide

Saint-Quay-Portrieux lies ahead: pass Plage du Châtelet and a seawater swimming pool. Walk down to Boulevard du Général de Gaulle, beside Plage du Casino.

SAINT-QUAY-PORTRIEUX

Sailors from Saint-Quay-Portrieux were active in the cod fisheries around Newfoundland and, later, Iceland. Saint-Quay-Portrieux is now one of the leading ports for harvesting *coquilles Saint-Jacques* (scallops); with Erquy and Paimpol, it hosts in alternate years the Fête de la Coquille Saint-Jacques.

As French painters in the late 19th century broke from academic traditions and (among other innovations) created their art in the open air, the landscapes and light of Brittany attracted them. Among the artists who visited Saint-Quay-Portrieux and painted here were Berthe Morisot, Eugène Boudin and Paul Signac.

High tide refreshes the water in Saint-Quay's swimming pool

STAGE 13
Saint-Quay-Portrieux to Bréhec

Start	Saint-Quay-Portrieux
Finish	Bréhec
Distance	20km
Ascent	940m
Descent	935m
Time	5hr 15min
Maps	IGN TOP25 0916OT, 0814OT
Refreshments	Cafés/restaurants at Saint-Marc, Port Goret, Le Palus, Bréhec
Transport	BreizhGo line 1
Accommodation	Hotels and/or *chambres d'hôtes* in Le Palus, Plouha, Bréhec; campground in Lanloup (1km off GR34)

This stage offers great views of the sea on a trail that descends and climbs steep slopes enclosing narrow coves. There are also unique highlights: Gwin Zégal's wooden stake port and Plage Bonaparte, the scene of a successful operation involving British forces and the French Resistance during World War II.

In **Saint-Quay-Portrieux**, walk northwest on Boulevard du Général de Gaulle and turn right after the casino to follow the embankment beside Plage du Casino. At the end of that beach, walk up steps to a path that continues around the coast, with a short detour on a road to go around a building. The GR34 leaves the built-up area to follow a route close to the rocky cliffs and the sea: easy walking, but quite dramatic!

Turn inland to cross fields and woods. Turn right at a T-junction to walk on a path beside a road, passing the 15th-century Saint-Marc chapel. Turn right through a parking area leading to **Plage de Saint-Marc** (café). Pick up the GR34 at the end of the parking area and turn left to continue along the coast.

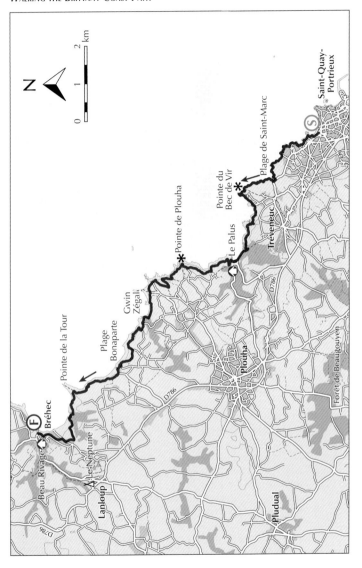

Cliffs north of Saint-Quay-Portrieux

About 1km from Saint-Marc, the trail passes the narrow **Pointe du Bec de Vir** and continues down to Port Goret (**1hr 15min**). ▶ Walk through Port Goret's parking area (café/restaurant) and continue straight through a grassy area to a trail. Upon reaching a road, turn right and (after 100 metres) left on a path that climbs into open country above the coastal cliffs.

Follow a broad path as it descends in a forest. Turn right at a T-junction beside a stone wall and walk to **Palus beach**: turn left and walk to the end of the beach, where there are cafés/restaurants and a hotel. ▶ Le Palus is a good place to pause, because you now have some climbing to do...

Walk up the steps to the right of the cafés/restaurants and continue uphill on a path through a hairpin right turn. The trail levels off in open country, then enters dense vegetation and climbs further. The reward for this climbing – reaching 100m above sea level near **Pointe de Plouha**, the highest coastal cliff in Brittany – is a dramatic view over the sea. The Cap Fréhel lighthouse is visible on the horizon, 40km away (**2hr 30min**).

About 4km from Le Palus, pass a parking area with a side-trail toward Pointe du Pommier and a sign referring to the Sentier des Falaises (cliff trail). The GR34 reaches

A side-trail leads to Pointe du Bec de Vir, with views worthy of the map table here and a bench from which to admire it all.

A road leads from here to Plouha (4km).

105

a road and makes a dogleg left/right turn to continue straight on a trail. But before that, consider turning right on the road to descend 350 metres to **Gwin Zégal** – it's worth the detour.

> The **port à pieux de bois** (wooden stake port) at Gwin Zégal presents a manner of mooring boats that dates back to the Middle Ages. Oaken tree trunks, about 15 metres in length, are buried in the sand with rocks to stabilise them. These trunks, projecting some 10 metres above the ground, are mooring posts for boats. The length of the trunks allows boats to rise and settle with the tide.

Ahead lies Port Moguer, a narrow gap in the cliffs leading to the beach that extends west from Gwin Zégal. The GR34 descends in a forest to a road, crosses it and climbs the opposite slope. You emerge from dense vegetation on a level trail in open country.

Pass massive pine trees just before joining a road that leads to a T-junction: turn right here on a road that soon leads to a trail through fields. Pass a monument commemorating the Réseau Shelburne (Shelburne Network) and turn right on a trail beside a bench, just before a parking area, to descend to **Plage Bonaparte** (**4hr**). A tunnel carved through the rock after the war now gives easy access to the beach itself.

> In 1944, the French Resistance worked with Britain's MI9 and Royal Navy to evacuate 135 Allied airmen from Anse Cochat, code-named 'Plage Bonaparte'. The airmen were hidden in safe houses until motor gunboats operating from Dartmouth could approach the coast to take them off the beach. They carried out eight successful evacuations without being detected by a German artillery unit on nearby Pointe de la Tour. This was the famous **Shelburne Network**.

Walk through the Plage Bonaparte parking area and continue up a forest trail. Make a right turn soon. Then, 1.5km further, the way forks: the rugged trail to the right goes out to **Pointe de la Tour**, while the GR34 follows the left fork. The route goes up and down, reaching a T-junction with another trail. Turn right here, descend to a small beach and climb a steep slope on the other side.

At the top of the climb, the trail emerges in open country and Bréhec comes into sight. Continue on a road to an intersection with another trail (GR34A); turn right here and walk along a sunken path carved in rock – a former railway line.

Turn right at a T-junction on a road that leads to a parking area in **Bréhec**. Turn left here on a road that passes through a residential area and becomes a dirt path in woods. Finally, the trail reaches steps on the right. Turn left here (off the GR34) to walk up to Route de la Corniche, where there is a *chambres d'hôtes*, or continue on the GR34 down the steps to the beach, where there has been accommodation in the past (check for up-to-date information), along with cafés/restaurants.

Plage Bonaparte in peace time; Pointe de la Tour, the rocky headland where a German artillery unit was stationed in 1944, is visible in the middle distance

STAGE 14
Bréhec to Paimpol

Start	Bréhec
Finish	Paimpol (harbour)
Distance	21km
Ascent	625m
Descent	635m
Time	5hr 45min
Map	IGN TOP25 0814OT
Refreshments	Cafés/restaurants in Kerity, Paimpol
Transport	BreizhGo line 1; railway service in Paimpol
Accommodation	Hotels and/or *chambres d'hôtes* in Kerity, Paimpol

This stage combines level, easy walking with some short but steep climbs and descents. There is also variety in the terrain: open country and forests. The nearby sea is not always visible, but the elevation of the coastal trail offers good views in the open areas. Be sure to carry food and water upon departure, as there are no refreshments along the trail before the approach to Paimpol.

This stage begins at steps opposite **Bréhec**'s beach, near the end of the row of cafés and restaurants. The steps lead to a trail with good views back over Bréhec. Walk up the trail to a road. Turn right and walk beside this quiet road for 1.5km, then follow a signed trail on the right downhill. Pass (or perhaps pause at) a bench with a splendid view over the switchbacks of the trail that you will climb after this descent.

At the bottom of the steep descent, turn left in a parking area and immediately right to reach a trail that climbs those switchbacks that you admired from the opposite slope. After the climb, continue on a trail that leads to a T-junction with a road. Turn right here and, after 150 metres, turn right at another T-junction toward Pointe de Minard.

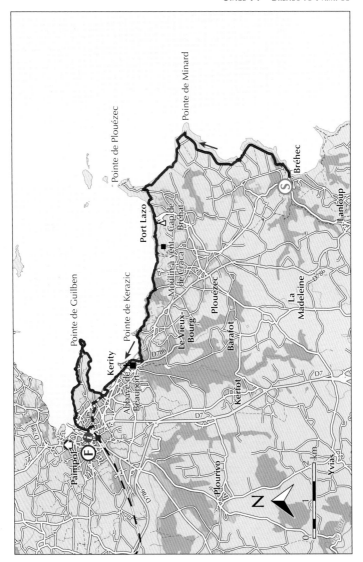

Just before **Pointe de Minard**, turn left on a broad trail (**1hr 30min**). The trail follows the coast through open country with colourful gorse covering the land during the spring. After walking briefly on a dirt road, descend a steep trail to Porz Donan and climb back up the opposite slope. After that climb, walk along a pleasant trail to a T-junction with a road.

A right turn here leads to Pointe de Plouézec.

Turn left and walk 100 metres on the road. ◄ Pass the entrance to 'Sculptures en Liberté' (an open-air display of works by the Breton sculptor Kito) and continue on a trail in the woods. Descend to a parking area, turn right on Route du Cap Horn and follow this road where it forks right to **Port Lazo**. After 500 metres on this road, turn right on a trail just before a picnic table with a good view over the bay toward Paimpol (**2hr 30min**).

Over the next 4km, the trail remains close to the coast, generally in forest but with passages across open land. You begin with a descent from the road. Where the trail levels off, make a hairpin left turn. It is easy walking from here, with gentle slopes. A side-trail on the left leads to the **Moulin à vent de Craca**, a restored 19th-century windmill that welcomes visitors during the summer. About one kilometre further, descend to a road: turn right here, walk through a parking area and continue on a trail to the left.

Finally, after walking through forest and field (with steps up and down steep slopes), you come to a road: turn right here, walk 200 metres on the road and then turn left on a trail toward **Pointe de Kerarzic**. The trail enters the protected estate of the Abbaye de Beauport, crosses a stream and passes the ruins of a water mill. The stark ruins of the abbey's Gothic church stand on the left (**4hr**).

Premonstratensian canons (the 'White Canons') established **Beauport Abbey** in the 13th century. The abbey, already in decline, was closed and sold in several lots during the French Revolution. The Conservatoire du Littoral (coastal protection agency) purchased Beauport Abbey in 1992 and carried out restoration work. The abbey today is not

only a place for tourists to visit but also a cultural centre.

Beauport Abbey

The GR34 now follows a path close to the water through **Kerity**, with numerous benches and picnic tables. The trail forks at a pond: follow the right fork, turn left at the end of the pond and cross a small dyke beside an old tidal mill. Turn right on Rue de Kerlégan and immediately curve right on a path beside the Base de loisirs de Poulafret (a sports centre) toward Pointe de Guilben. ▶

To short-cut to the centre of Paimpol, continue straight on Rue de Kerlégan, go left on Rue Salvador Allende leading to Rue Anatole Le Braz, then right on Rue du Général Leclerc and right on Rue de Labenne.

The path passes a boat ramp and is mostly hemmed in by hedges, but there are occasional views over the water to the other side of the bay where you walked a short while ago. Walk around **Pointe de Guilben** through a grove of trees with open space allowing you to appreciate this beautiful setting (**5hr**).

For the final stretch to Paimpol, follow a trail to the right of a majestic, multi-trunked tree. This trail on the northern side of the promontory is more scenic, closer to the sea than the southern trail. After 2km, the trail reaches the first homes: follow a gravel road, turn right on Rue du Tumulus, right at a T-junction and finally left on a path beside the beach. Follow this path and curve left to reach the harbour in **Paimpol**.

PAIMPOL

Paimpol remembers a history of fishing for cod that dates back more than 500 years. The value of the fisheries made them a contested element of international rivalries. In the Treaty of Utrecht (1713), France recognised British sovereignty over Newfoundland, but retained rights for its fishermen to fish in these waters and to occupy temporary structures for drying fish along specified sections of the coast. Later, there were disagreements over the interpretation of these rights. Finally, as part of the package of agreements known as the Entente Cordiale (1904), France renounced its fishing rights derived from the Treaty of Utrecht. In return, Britain agreed to the modification in France's favour of certain boundaries of their respective colonies in Africa.

Meanwhile, the *grande pêche* for cod in waters around Iceland had developed. The Icelandic fishery was profitable for many ship-owners, but dangerous for the fishermen, most of whom were recruited from nearby villages and farms. It is estimated that 120 ships and 2000 men were lost during the years of the *grande pêche*.

This cultural heritage is present in Paimpol today: in addition to the annual Fête des Islandais et des Terre-Neuvas (literally: Icelanders and Newfoundlanders Festival) in July, the Festival du Chant de Marin (Sea Shanty Festival) is held biennially in August (odd-numbered years). Paimpol also hosts the Fête de la Coquille Saint-Jacques in April, alternating with Erquy and Saint-Quay-Portrieux. The Musée de la Mer (Museum of the Sea) is worth a visit for those interested in the Atlantic fisheries.

Paimpol's inner harbour

STAGE 15

Paimpol to Lézardrieux

Start	Paimpol
Finish	Lézardrieux (centre)
Distance	25km
Ascent	655m
Descent	635m
Time	5hr 45min
Map	IGN TOP25 0814OT
Refreshments	Cafés/restaurants in Porz Even, Pointe de l'Arcouest, Loguivy-de-la-Mer, Lézardrieux
Transport	BreizhGo lines 25, 27; railway service in Paimpol
Accommodation	Hotels and/or *chambres d'hôtes* in Porz Even, Pointe de l'Arcouest, Loguivy-de-la-Mer, Lézardrieux

This stage comprises two contrasting parts: from Paimpol to Loguivy-de-la-Mer, the GR34 goes through several villages on a placid trail. After Loguivy-de-la-Mer, the trail crosses hilly, wooded terrain where there are no villages until the approach to Lézardrieux. A historical note adds spice to this stage: you'll be walking in the footsteps of Vladimir Lenin!

From the harbour in **Paimpol**, walk west on Quai Duguay-Trouin and turn right on Quai Morand. At the end of the quay, turn left to walk along a tree-lined path. A monument here pays tribute to merchant seamen who joined Free French Forces during World War II. At the end of the embankment, turn right and then left on a road, passing a shipyard on the right. Where that road curves left, turn right on a narrow path that leads to a road and a small parking lot. ▸

If high tide floods the beach ahead, turn left on this road, right on the main road (D789) and right again after 1km onto Route de Traou Nod.

Walk through the parking lot; continue in woods and through marshlands. After a short walk on a trail beside the beach, continue straight on a surfaced road. (The high-tide variant rejoins the main route here.) Pass a *gîte* and continue on a trail into the woods where the road

The Mur des Disparus-en-mer in Ploubazlanec's cemetery honours the memory of sailors lost at sea.

curves left. This is Chemin de la Grève; it becomes a sur-faced road and passes through a village, Kerroc'h.

Continue straight on Rue de Kerroc'h. The 18th-century **Calvaire Cornic** stands in a crossroads; a nearby panel explains its iconography. Follow Rue de Kerroc'h to the right and fork left on Chemin de Kergaud. This road passes though woods as a dirt path and is then surfaced again in a residential area of Ploubazlanec. ◄ Turn left on Rue des Pêcheurs d'Islande, which leads to an intersec-tion dominated by the Perros Hamon Chapel.

Make a sharp right turn on Impasse Guillaume Le Rousseau and turn right after 100 metres onto a small lane. Descend steps on the right and turn left on a road. After a short walk, turn right on a narrow path bordered

Calvaire Cornic in Ploubazlanec

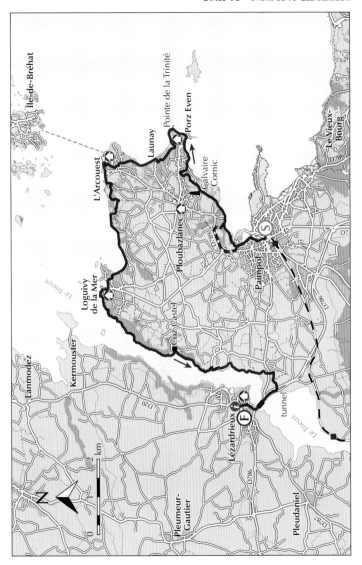

Île-de-Bréhat

Pointe de la Trinité

Porz Even

Launay

L'Arcouest

Galvaire Cornic

Ploubazlanec

Le Trieux

Loguivy de la Mer

Coz Castel

Paimpol

Lanmodez

Kermouster

Le Trieux

tunnel

Lézardrieux

Le Vieux-Bourg

D786

D7

D789

D786

D789

Pleumeur-Gautier

D20

D786

Pleudaniel

D787

km

N

by a white fence. The path leads to the coastal trail and then a road to **Porz Even** (**1hr 30min**). After passing a *chambres d'hôtes*, turn left toward Chapelle de la Trinité.

The route goes around **Pointe de la Trinité**; follow a pleasant trail in the woods. Upon reaching a road, turn right and immediately right again down another trail. This leads to a road. Walk along this road for 1.5km, turning right at a fork amid beautiful stone buildings in **Launay** to reach a beach.

Turn left to walk beside this beach, then right beside the Maison de la Réserve Paule Lapicque. Follow the trail across a road and continue on Chemin Pierre et Marie Curie. Turn right at a T-junction and left beside an impressive stone building on a narrow path called Gardenn ar Spern Du.

Cross a large intersection and go straight on Chemin du Rohu. Turn left on a dead-end road where a sign points to Le Rohu and the Sentier de l'Embarcadère. This leads to a pleasant path that descends in a forest to **l'Arcouest**. A short distance to the right is the *embarcadère* (pier) for boats to Île de Bréhat, while the GR34 turns left here.

> **Île de Bréhat** is actually two islands, linked by an old bridge. The Gulf Stream gives Bréhat a temperate climate that favours vegetation such as eucalyptus, fig trees and mimosa on the southern island. The landscape of the northern island is more typically Breton, with heathland crowned by a lighthouse standing over a wild, rocky coast.

Walk beside the road, passing a monument in honour of Irène and Frédéric Joliot-Curie, Nobel Prize laureates who spent vacations in Arcouest. Fork right and walk through a parking area, then turn right on a trail beside the beach. Turn left on a road, right on a dirt road after a beautiful stone house, and finally left on a narrow trail that climbs in a forest.

The trail broadens in open country, offering beautiful views over the water. After a steep descent in woods, turn left on a road. Walk beside this road while it remains close to the coast. Continue straight on a path where the road curves to the left. This path and – after 1km – a road lead to **Loguivy-de-la-Mer**, a town with an attractive little harbour (**3hr 30min**).

> Loguivy-de-la-Mer has a long history as a pleasant place for a holiday. In 1902, **Vladimir Lenin** spent a month here with his mother, his sister Anna and her three children. He needed a break from his political activities. In a letter to a comrade, Lenin reported: 'I liked it here very much on the whole and have had a good rest…' Imagine Lenin wearing an early 20th-century bathing costume and a big straw hat, relaxing with a book in a deckchair beside the beach – a bourgeois interlude before he got back to the Revolution…

Arriving in Loguivy, cross Rue de Beg ar Enez, descend steps to Rue de la Jetée and turn left to walk beside the harbour. Pass a parking lot and turn right, left at a T-junction and right on a narrow path where a sign ('Passage Privé') bars the way straight ahead. This path turns left at a beach and becomes a road that curves left. Shortly after that curve, turn right on a trail where a sign points to Lézardrieux. Walk down steps to a trail behind a sailing school building. Watch for a left turn through a gap in the fence beside this trail.

The GR34 now follows the eastern side of the Trieux estuary for more than 6km – mostly in forest; sometimes above the water, sometimes beside it. Sections of the trail are steep with steps. Early on, you will clamber over an outcrop of boulders facing Roche aux Oiseaux. Later, the trail settles down in a level walk beside the water, which is pleasant after those steps.

After a short walk on a beach, turn left on a boat ramp and continue on a dyke to reach **Coz Castel** (3.5km from Loguivy). Follow a trail behind the buildings and descend to a boat landing; walk across the landing and up a road on the opposite side. Leave the road after 250 metres on a trail that climbs in the woods. The trail levels off beside a wall, then descends to the right. The trail soon narrows and reverts to going up and down steeply. Curve right past an old *lavoir* (washhouse) and continue straight across a road, entering a residential area (**5hr**).

Walk up Chemin du Porjou and turn right at a T-junction on Chemin de Kerivon. Follow this road and walk through a tunnel into a parking area. Pick up a trail at the lower end of the parking area to the right. This trail leads to a dirt road that climbs to the main road just before a bridge over the Trieux River. Cross the **bridge** on a walkway on its left side.

Cross the main road at a zebra crossing 100 metres beyond the bridge and continue straight on Rue Saint-Christophe toward the centre of **Lézardrieux**. A hotel that warmly welcomes GR34 hikers is located on this street.

> **Lézardrieux** boasts an elegant 18th-century church with two towers flanking a steeple with arcades supporting its bells. The World War I monument behind the church features a dramatic, polychromatic statue of a dying soldier and a defiant Gallic rooster. A music festival, Trieux Tonic Blues, is staged in Lézardrieux each year over the Ascension Day weekend in May.

Lézardrieux's church

STAGE 16
Lézardrieux to Le Québo

Start	Lézardrieux
Finish	Le Québo (beside Sillon de Talbert)
Distance	19km
Ascent	315m
Descent	335m
Time	5hr
Map	IGN TOP25 0814OT
Refreshments	*Crêperie* in Kermouster; cafés/restaurants in l'Armor, le Québo
Transport	BreizhGo line 25
Accommodation	*Chambres d'hôtes* in Lanmodez (1.5km), l'Armor; Laneros campground

After the hilly terrain of the right bank of the Trieux estuary, this walk along the left bank is easy, without strenuous climbs and descents. The views over the water are not so dramatic here, but the sea opens beautifully before you at le Québo, next to an interesting geographical feature, the Sillon de Talbert.

Walk north on Rue Saint-Christophe (which becomes Rue des Écoles) to a T-junction in the centre of **Lézardrieux**. Turn right to walk through Place du Centre toward the church.

Refreshments are sparse along the route of this stage (and the next stage), so you may wish to buy provisions before leaving Lézardrieux. There is a supermarket on Rue du 8 mai 1945 to the left of the T-junction and a bakery in the Place du Centre.

Walk along the right side of the church and through the Square du Souvenir behind it, with its World War I

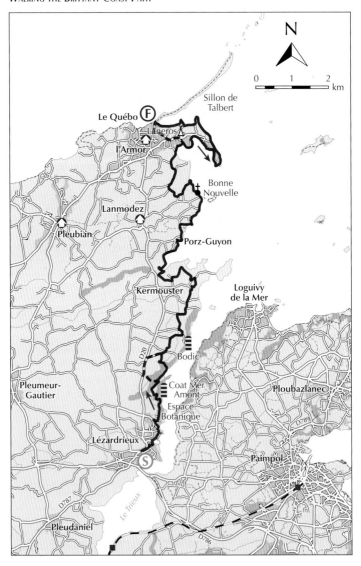

monument. Turn left through a parking lot to a signposted trail down steps leading to the harbour. Turn left and walk around the harbour.

Continue on Rue du Trieux as it climbs and curves left, passing the lantern room of a 19th-century light-house on display. The GR34 soon leaves this road by descending steps to the right, then turning left on a road that leads back to Rue du Trieux.

After a few steps on Rue du Trieux, make a hair-pin right turn on Rue des Perdrix toward the **Espace Botanique**. The tarmac soon ends as you enter open country. The dirt road descends in a forest; continue straight on a trail into the Espace Botanique when the road turns. Panels beside the trail identify the plants and animals that inhabit the area.

The trail leaves the Espace Botanique on reaching a road: turn left here and right on a dirt path after pass-ing a white building with a prominent inscription: 'COAT MER AMONT'. This **lighthouse**, aligned with a lower one (Coat Mer Aval) on a bearing of 219 degrees, guides navi-gation on the river.

A field outside Lézardrieux

To avoid the beach ahead at high tide, turn left at the T-junction, walk 500 metres and turn right on a main road (D20). Follow for 500 metres, turn right and continue on this road for 400 metres to rejoin the GR34.

The high-tide variant rejoins the main route here.

Follow the path to a road: turn left, then right at a T-junction with another road, Rue du Moulin à Mer. ◄ Pass the tidal mill that gave this road its name and an old stone dyke. Continue on a rocky beach, then on a dyke beside the river. Walk briefly through the woods (or continue on the beach at low tide). Back on the beach, turn left to walk up a trail into the woods. The coast may seem remote as you climb in this dense, humid forest with large ferns and bamboo. You are unlikely to hear the screeching of herring gulls here!

Pass an old *lavoir* and turn right on a road beside a stone house. The road curves left and continues in open country. Turn right at a T-junction with a road. ◄ Just 100 metres further, turn right at another T-junction and immediately left on a path. The path passes through a group of farm buildings to reach a surfaced road.

Turn right and walk on the road, with the striking form of the **Bodic lighthouse** (resembling the Space Shuttle) standing over the fields to the right. Turn left after 400 metres onto a dirt road. Walk up this road (bearing left at a fork) and turn right on a narrow trail that becomes a surfaced road. Turn right on a road that leads to Kermouster (**1hr 45min**).

The GR34 winds its way through **Kermouster**: first right on a gravel road opposite a *crêperie* and left on a grass path, then up a road to a hairpin right turn on a grass path to a surfaced road among buildings, and finally left on a road at a T-junction. Turn right at a roundabout and continue on a narrow lane.

The path broadens, turns left and becomes a dirt road. Turn left on a surfaced road and, within 100 metres, right on a path into fields. Bear right on a road after 300 metres and continue in the same direction on a trail down to a dirt path, where you turn right. After 200 metres, turn left on a trail that descends to a small cove.

Pass an attractive stone cottage and curve right on a road beside a stream. The GR34 leaves the road where a sign bars access to private property and warns of a dog, descending on a trail to another road: walk 130 metres on this road and follow a trail on the right that stays close to the water.

At an intersection, turn right to walk through a village, **Porz-Guyon** (**2hr 30min**), then turn right on a dirt road toward the water. ▶ Turn left on the coastal trail to walk 100 metres on a beach, left off the beach on a road and immediately right on a trail above the beach.

The path crosses a road (the high-tide variant rejoins the main route here) and passes the **Bonne Nouvelle chapel** inside its wall. Turn left 600 metres after the chapel and leave the coast on a road among houses. Turn right after 500 metres on another road toward a cylindrical stone tower (formerly a windmill). Continue on a dirt lane past the tower and turn right at two successive T-junctions.

Go left toward l'Armor and Pleubian where the road forks. Follow this road as it curves right and go straight on a dirt path where the road curves left. The path forks after 350 metres (**3hr 45min**); there are two ways to reach le Québo from here.

One option is to turn right and follow the route of the GR34 around the long, narrow peninsula that extends to the southeast. Near the tip of the peninsula, you'll pass an industrial plant that processes seaweed collected from local beaches (for production of cosmetics, etc). The route on the north side of the peninsula leads to the Maison du Sillon in **Le Québo**.

Alternatively, go left at the fork and walk through **l'Armor**. Turn left at a T-junction on Rue de Laneros, fork right on Rue Run Traou, continue on Rue du Québo and turn right on Rue du Sillon du Talbert to reach the Maison du Sillon in **Le Québo**. This second alternative is recommended, as is the addition of a walk on the **Sillon de Talbert**, which is more interesting than walking around the peninsula, to end this stage.

The **Sillon de Talbert** is a shingle bank that extends about 3km from the shore. It was formed by the combined action of rivers on the two sides of the peninsula, Trieux and Jaudy. The Sillon moves

If the beach ahead is submerged, walk north 130 metres on the road, then turn right on a road that leads to the coast to rejoin the GR34.

The base of the Sillon de Talbert

under the effects of currents, tides and winds, and it is fragile; it was 4.5km long in the 18th century. In March 2018, a breech opened in the Sillon. (Currently, therefore, you cannot walk the entire length of the Sillon at high tide.) The Sillon is a protected habitat for birds that nest and rest here. The pebbles themselves are protected; collecting them is prohibited.

STAGE 17
Le Québo to Tréguier

Start	Le Québo (beside Sillon de Talbert)
Finish	Tréguier (centre)
Distance	20km
Ascent	365m
Descent	360m
Time	5hr 45min
Map	IGN TOP25 0814OT
Refreshments	None before Tréguier
Transport	BreizhGo lines 25, 27
Accommodation	*Chambres d'hôtes* in Kermagen, Pleubian (2km off GR34); hotels, *chambres d'hôtes* in Tréguier

The first part of this stage stays close to the coast: easy, relaxed walking in a pleasant setting, passing several small beaches along the way. The route moves inland on tarmac during the latter part of this stage but descends for a walk on the shore beside the Jaudy River before the final approach to Tréguier.

From **le Québo**, pick up the GR34 behind the restaurant at the base of the Sillon de Talbert. Follow a trail southwest above the beach. Pass a playground at Porz Ran, leave the beach to the left and walk up a few steps to the coastal path in front of a group of houses. The GR34 follows this pleasant trail with a brief passage inland. Pass an old **lighthouse** at Port La Chaine and walk along a long shingle bank. At Crec'h Costiou you reach a parking area near **Kermagen** (**1hr**).

Continue along the coast behind a breakwater of large rectangular stones. Pass Crec'h Peuillart (nearly 2km from Kermagen) and (1km further) **Port Béni**. ▶ Walk 150 metres on a road south from Port Béni and veer left on a trail where the tarmac ends. Turn right at a T-junction and walk 500 metres on a surfaced road, then turn right on a dirt road.

A panel here describes veins of Icartian metamorphic gneiss – the oldest rock in France, formed 1800–2000 million years ago – within granite that is a mere 600 million years old.

125

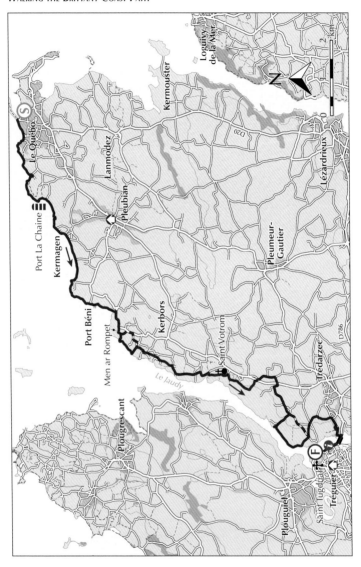

Where the dirt road forks, continue straight between the two roads on a path through dense vegetation to another dirt road. ▶ Turn left here and walk a short distance to a surfaced road. At high tide, turn left on this road to follow a waymarked variant. Otherwise, turn right and walk to a beach (**2hr 15min**).

Turn left and enjoy a 600-metre walk on the beach. Where a GR mark on a rock points the way, turn left to follow a trail (soon a road) off the beach. Leave the tarmac on a path to the right 200 metres from the beach. (The high-tide variant rejoins the main route here.) Follow the path as it turns toward the water, turn left on a road and (after 100 metres) right on another road that leads to a trail in the woods.

Turn right after 350 metres to walk a short distance on a road that descends toward the water and go left on a dirt path. On reaching a crossroads, turn right and then left on a road shortly before reaching the water. Tréguier comes into view at the head of the Jaudy estuary.

Walk 1.2km on this road. Turn sharply right at a fork as the road descends, and then left on a dirt path that climbs back up, leading to a pleasant trail. Turn left on a dirt road at a T-junction, walk past the small stone **Chapelle de Saint Votrom**, and turn right on surfaced road at a T-junction.

Continue straight on a dirt path after the road curves left. Pass a group of farm buildings and curve left past the entrance to a large manor house. Cross a main road and immediately turn right on a smaller road. Turn right after 500 metres on another road that takes you back across the main road. Turn left after 200 metres and walk 1km to an intersection, where signs point to options (**3hr 30min**).

It is helpful to know the state of the tide, since the beach is not visible from here: around high tide, continue straight for 800 metres to meet the low-tide route on the right. (This route is shown as a variant on the map.) Around low tide, turn right at the intersection, walk 400 metres down the road and follow a trail that branches left. At the bottom of this trail, turn left to walk along a path among the trees beside the rocky shore. The trail soon

Turn right here for Men ar Rompet, a Neolithic dolmen. It's just 200 metres – worth the detour.

drops to the beach, which may be quite muddy. Trees hang over your path; seaweed caught in their branches shows how high the tide can rise here. After 1km, leave the beach on a road to the left. The road climbs gently, curves left and meets the high-tide variant. Veer right (east) on a diagonal here.

Walk to a T-junction and turn right; continue straight through an intersection. Turn right after 250 metres on a dirt road and right at a T-junction on a surfaced road. A GR mark indicates a right turn on Rue de Cre'ch Urustal, which soon returns to the main road. Descend to the river.

Turn left, then right to cross the **bridge** over the Jaudy to Tréguier. Turn right after the bridge. Follow the GR34 on Rue du Port beside the river, or turn left through Place du Général de Gaulle and continue on Rue St André to reach the centre of **Tréguier**.

TRÉGUIER

The procession of the Grand Pardon de Saint Yves leaves Tréguier's Saint-Tugdual Cathedral

Tréguier is an attractive town. Half-timbered houses line narrow streets in its centre. Its majestic cathedral is dedicated to Saint Tugdual, a Welsh monk who was one of Brittany's Founder Saints. Tréguier's best-known religious figure is Saint Yves. Yves Hélory de Kermartin (1253–1308) studied law and became an ecclesiastical judge. He lived an ascetic life and demonstrated great sympathy for the poor: *'Sanctus Ivo erat Brito, advocatus et non latro, res mirando populo'* ('Saint Yves was a Breton and a lawyer, but not a thief, a remarkable thing in people's eyes'). Yves is the patron saint of lawyers, many of whom participate in the Grand Pardon de Saint Yves on the third Sunday of May. The procession of the Pardon leaves the Cathedral and passes a statue of Ernest Renan in the Place du Martray. Renan (1823–1893) was a philologist whose rational, analytical approach to Christianity provoked anger among traditionalist Catholics. When this statue of Renan was inaugurated in 1903, troops had to be summoned to quell a riot by a crowd of outraged traditionalists.

STAGE 18

Tréguier to Port Blanc

Start	Tréguier
Finish	Port Blanc
Distance	29.5km
Ascent	525m
Descent	525m
Time	8hr 15min
Maps	IGN TOP25 0814OT, 0714OT
Refreshments	Cafés/restaurants in Plouguiel, La Roche Jaune, Plougrescant, Porz Hir, Kermerrien, Port Blanc
Transport	TILT line M (Thursdays)
Accommodation	*Chambres d'hôtes* in Plougrescant, Gouermel, Bugélès; campground in Porz Hir; hotel, a *chambres d'hôtes*, campground in Port Blanc

The first half of this stage is a pleasant walk down the estuary of the Jaudy River; sometimes on the beach, sometimes on forest trails, but starting with a long stretch of tarmac. Then you pass Porz Hir and enter another world on the other side of this peninsula: the trail is still easy, close to the seashore, but awesome boulders introduce the Côte de Granit Rose.

Leaving from the centre of **Tréguier**, descend Boulevard Anatole le Braz. Rejoin the GR34 just before Pont Noir and make a hairpin left turn. Walk past a parking area for recreational vehicles, branch right and continue through a passage under a stone viaduct. Turn right and follow the river to an elegant suspension footbridge, **Passerelle Saint-François** (built in 1834; re-built in 2013). Cross the river here and turn left on a broad, shaded path, then continue on a road.

Turn right at a T-junction on La Vielle Côte and right again after 200 metres to walk up Rue de Tréguier. Turn left and continue straight on Garden Kerber when Rue de

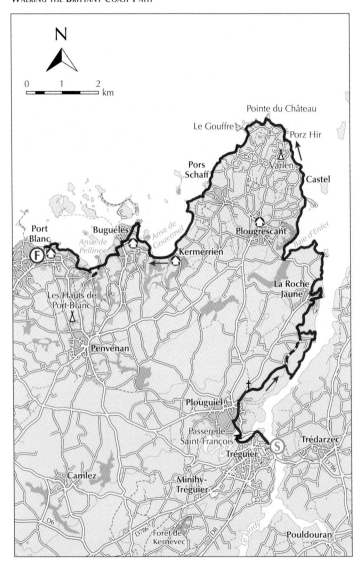

Tréguier curves left. Turn right after 200 metres. At a fork, where a cross stands between the roads, bear right. Turn right 1.5km after that fork on Crec'h Sulliet, a small road that descends to the river (**1hr 15min**). ▶

Turn left to walk beside the river, first on a rocky shore (slippery when wet), then on a smooth dirt surface. On reaching a road, turn right and immediately left back to the beach. Leave the beach after 200 metres on a trail to the left that climbs into a forest and levels off in open country. Turn left on a dirt road at a T-junction and right on a surfaced road. ▶

Walk 1km and then make a succession of turns while enjoying beautiful views over the river: right on Rue de Palamos, left on Rue de Gralange, left on Rue Gader Min, a left fork and finally a hairpin right turn on Rue du Port to enter **La Roche Jaune** (**2hr 15min**).

The road approaches the river. Just before a restaurant, turn left on a path that climbs steeply. Turn right on a dirt path after a short distance and continue on a surfaced road. Turn left at a T-junction on Rue Belvédère and follow this road to an intersection. Turn right on Rue de l'Estuaire and, 400 metres further, right on a dirt road toward the river. Branch left on a trail toward the beach.

Walk along a trail beside the water, alternating between forest and open country. On reaching a dirt road, turn left and then right on a pleasant trail with water on the right and crops growing in fields on the left. The trail reaches a road at the head of a cove called **Baie de l'Enfer** (**3hr 15min**): turn right, walk a short distance on the road and then go right on a trail that continues down the other side of the cove. ▶

The route from here is a delightful walk in the woods. After 2km, the trail descends steps to a beach and turns left to climb other steps back to the woods. (You can continue on the beach if the tide permits.) On reaching a small harbour, Beg ar Villin, turn left and walk to a surfaced road. Turn left here and then right just before an oyster facility. Continue on a trail beside the coast to **Castel**.

Around high tide, do not turn right on Crec'h Sulliet; continue straight for 1km on the main road to follow the variant shown on the map.

The high-tide variant rejoins the main route here.

Go straight on this road to reach Plougrescant (1km).

A side-trail 1.5km after Castel leads to the Varlen campground in Porz Hir.

Walk past Castel's beach and then up a road between buildings. Turn right on the coastal trail. ◄ A beautiful beach and harbour soon come into view: **Porz Hir**. Turn left and then right on a road that leads to an embankment above the beach. Continue straight on a smooth and easy path. The path curves left, passing **Pointe du Château**, and enters a forest with large boulders. Bear left to return to the coastal trail.

The house squeezed between two enormous rocks is Castel Meur (1861).

Pass a cone-shaped stone building to reach the Maison du Littoral, with educational exhibits and tourist information (**4hr 30min**). ◄ The GR34 turns left here, but a path to the right makes a loop to and from **Le Gouffre**, a towering rock formation that forms a chasm at the water's edge where waves crash against the rocks. It's well worth the short detour.

The path after the Maison du Littoral leads to a road: turn right here and right again on a dirt path after passing a house. Continue in open country along a coast, Crec'h Mélo, that is strewn with boulders of all sizes. About 3km from the Maison du Littoral, pass **Pors Scaff** and walk along an embankment. Curve left on a road after a group of buildings and right at a fork. Continue on a road past Rojo Wenn beach and turn right 100 metres after the beach on a gravel path.

Castel Meur: no complaints about the neighbours!

Follow the coast to reach a causeway at the head of **Anse de Gouermel** (there's a restaurant here at **Kermerrien** and a *gîte d'étape* 500 metres away). Walk

along the causeway, turn right on a small gravel road and right again on a forest trail. Continue on this trail, passing side-trails on the right leading to the beach.

Hikers beside Crec'h Mélo

After emerging from the forest, walk in an arc to the left around a beach. The latter part of this arc is a broad path and then rocky beach. Leave the beach to walk through a small clearing, followed by a short walk on another beach to a road.

Turn left on Rue du Port and walk into **Buguélès** (**7hr**). Turn right after 600 metres onto Venelle Saint-Nicolas and right at a T-junction on Rue Ambroise Thomas. The road curves left to a T-junction with Rue Castel Coz. Turn left here, descend to an intersection and turn right on Rue de l'Île Marquer beside an old water fountain. Walk up this road and turn left on Rue des Mouettes. Make a hairpin right turn onto Rue de Guernotier to leave the town.

The road crosses a tidal flat at the head of **Anse de Pellinec**. ▶ Turn right on Rue de la Pellinec and right on Chemin de la Marine. Leave this road after 50 metres on a trail to the right. Walk to the coast, turn left and continue beside the water to **Port Blanc**. Pass through a parking area beside the harbour and walk on a path beside a road. Turn right onto a road that leads to the Grand Hotel – a convenient place to finish this stage.

At high tide, follow the trail marked 'Passage par marée haute', shown on the map.

STAGE 19
Port Blanc to Perros-Guirec

Start	Port Blanc
Finish	Perros-Guirec (Rue Anatole Le Braz)
Distance	15km
Ascent	255m
Descent	250m
Time	3hr 45min
Map	IGN TOP25 0714OT
Refreshments	Cafés/restaurants in Trestel, Port l'Épine, Louannec, Pont ar Sauz, Perros-Guirec
Transport	TILT lines E, Le Macareux
Accommodation	Hotels and/or *chambres d'hôtes* in Trestel, Port l'Épine, Louannec, Pont ar Sauz, Perros-Guirec

The scenery along this stage is not so spectacular as that of the previous stage (not to mention the next stage!), but this one offers easy and pleasant walking along the coast. Perros-Guirec, a lively city with vast, sandy beaches, is popular for family vacations.

A pointed rock stands offshore. It is surmounted by La Sentinelle, originally a lookout post, which was converted into an oratory early in the 20th century.

At low tide it is possible to walk on this beach to Trestel.

In **Port Blanc**, walk west on the embankment above the beach, parallel to Boulevard de la Mer. ◄ Pass a sailing centre to continue beside another beach. Where the road curves left, go straight on a surfaced path beside the rocky coast. It's a picturesque scene, with many small islands and large rocks close offshore. Follow a path on a dyke, then a sandy path beside it.

Pass a *poste de secours* and walk on a path between a **campground** and Plage des Dunes. One kilometre further, you reach another beach, **Plage du Royo**. ◄ Walk beside a road and continue straight on a path where the road curves left. Turn left after 250 metres and walk into a residential area of **Trestel**.

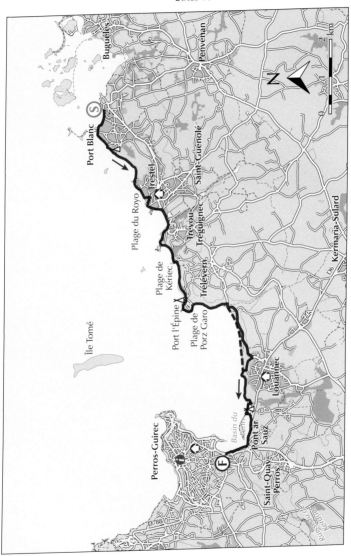

Coastal trail west of Port Blanc

Follow GR marks to a road that returns to the coast. (If you've walked on the beach, rejoin the GR34 here.) Walk past a white building on the right, Maison de l'Estran (a centre for children with disabilities), and then a large curved building on the left, the Centre de rééducation et de réadaptation fonctionnelles (a physical therapy centre).

Walk along the embankment beside Plage de Trestel. Near the end of the beach, continue on pavement beside a busy road. Turn right onto a smaller road after 250 metres. This road rises gently and descends to the beach at Port-le-Goff. Turn left and follow a path through bushes and past fields of grain.

On reaching a road, turn left and then turn right onto a road leading to **Plage de Kériec**. The trail follows the coast from here and joins a road to pass a campground in **Port l'Épine (1hr 45min)**. Walk through a parking lot and bear right where the road forks.

The GR34 follows this road around a small promontory, with views over the bay to Perros-Guirec and Île Tomé. After the road turns inland, watch for a right turn that leads down steps to another campground. On reaching a beach, turn left to walk beside the campground. The trail curves right along the coast above **Plage de Porz Garo**; sometimes in open country, sometimes in dense vegetation.

Turn right on a road (1km after the campground) toward a beach. Pass picnic tables and benches, walk through a small parking area and cross a footbridge to pick up a trail that enters the woods. The GR34 soon emerges from the woods to follow a main road. There is a bad section where the road climbs, as the verge is narrow or non-existent. ▶

Depending on the tide, you may be able to avoid this section by walking on the beach.

Finally, after 800 metres, leave this road by turning right on a small road and then immediately right on a narrow trail downhill in woods. Walk through a parking lot and turn right on a road toward the water (**2hr 45min**). Turn left onto a trail before reaching the beach for a pleasant walk in woods. Perros-Guirec is visible across the bay and getting closer.

Emerge from the woods after 1km and walk 100 metres to a road. Turn right here, then left on a path atop a stone dyke and through dunes, between the beach and a **campground**. When you reach the end of the campground, turn left on a road around the southern side of a pond, **Basin du Lenn**. Walk a short distance on the beach to **Pont ar Sauz** and turn right on a path that enters **Perros-Guirec**. ▶

A sign indicates with a pictogram that you should not use trekking poles with steel tips here.

The path follows what was a railway line to Rue Anatole Le Braz beside the harbour. While the historic centre of Perros-Guirec is inland, this area has accommodation and restaurants.

Perros-Guirec became a fashionable place for a seaside holiday around the turn of the 20th century. Maurice Denis, a leading painter in the post-impressionist Nabis group and the Symbolist movement, visited Perros-Guirec frequently and bought Villa Silencio here. A plaque on the villa records his appreciation: *'Jamais la nature ne m'a paru plus belle qu'à Perros'* ('Never has nature seemed more beautiful to me than in Perros'). Offshore is the Sept Îles bird sanctuary, home to an enormous population of northern gannets, as well as puffins and cormorants.

STAGE 20

Perros-Guirec to Trégastel (Coz Pors)

Start	Perros-Guirec
Finish	Trégastel (Coz Pors)
Distance	17.5km
Ascent	330m
Descent	325m
Time	4hr
Map	IGN TOP25 0714OT
Refreshments	Cafés/restaurants at Trestraou and Trestrignel beaches, Ploumanac'h, Trégastel
Transport	TILT lines E, Le Macareux
Accommodation	Hotels, *chambres d'hôtes* at Trestraou and Trestrignel beaches, Ploumanac'h, Coz Pors en Trégastel

This stage features the most spectacular scenery of the Côte de Granit Rose. A smooth, well-maintained path passes extraordinary pink granite boulders, on land and close offshore. There is easy access to the area by road and convenient parking nearby, so you will not be alone among these breathtaking rocks.

Walk north on Rue Anatole Le Braz beside **Perros-Guirec**'s harbour. Turn right on a path beside the harbour, with a pond on the left. Curve left beside the pond and then Boulevard de la Mer. The path continues beside the bay and follows the road up a gentle hill.

Fork right on Rue de Trestrignel. After 250 metres, fork right again on Rue de Pors ar Goret, a narrow lane that descends to a small beach. Walk 100 metres on the beach and leave it up steps into the woods.

On reaching a road, turn right and continue on a trail. Pass **Pointe du Château** and curve left to reach a road that descends to **Plage de Trestrignel**. Walk on the embankment above this beach and continue up a road

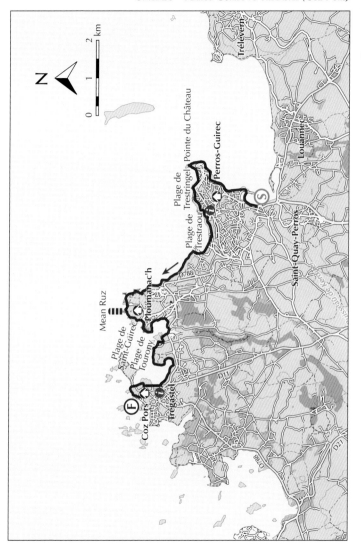

past a hotel. The road curves left and levels off in a residential area. Pass Square Per Jakez Helias, turn right on Venelle de Pors Nevez and immediately left on Venelle des Sept-Îles. Turn right after just 20 metres on a narrow path that leads to a road. Walk 100 metres on this road to a T-junction. Turn right here onto Rue des Sept-Îles and continue straight where the road merges into Rue du Maréchal Foch.

Walk down to **Plage de Trestraou** (**1hr 15min**). The embankment here is an animated place; cafés and restaurants, not to mention a casino, invite the walker to pause. Follow the embankment to the end of the beach. ◄ At a roundabout, walk up Rue de la Clarté where a sign points to the Sentier des Douaniers. Continue straight on a dirt path where the surfaced road curves left.

The next 4km are sublime – the heart of the Côte de Granit Rose. The paths in this protected natural site are broad and smooth. Here, again, the use of steel-tipped trekking poles is prohibited. While there are numerous side-trails leading to interesting rocks and beaches, the main trail is easy to follow (with occasional GR marks). You can relax on a bench along the trail and ponder the geological forces that created these enormous granite boulders, perched incongruously upon each other. ◄

In addition to the stunning natural beauty of this area, there are interesting human constructions: the Sémaphore de Ploumanac'h stands on a hill. Further on, you pass a small *guérite du douanier* (customs officer's hut) and a 17th-century *poudrière* (gunpowder magazine). The iconic Ploumanac'h lighthouse, **Mean Ruz**, pierces the horizon ahead of you.

> The original **lighthouse** was built of grey granite in 1860. It was rebuilt with pink granite in 1948 after its destruction during World War II. Opposite the lighthouse is the **Maison du Littoral**, well worth a visit to learn about the geology and history of this coast.
>
> A large, white structure houses an **SNSM rescue boat** that can be launched down a long ramp into

Boats for excursions to the Sept Îles bird sanctuary depart from a pier here.

Some of the rocks have whimsical names, such as the Wave, the Ram and Napoleon's Hat. A map published by the Maison du Littoral shows the location of many named boulders.

Ploumanac'h lighthouse

the water. The Société Nationale de Sauvetage en Mer (SNSM) is a non-profit association that undertakes rescue missions offshore, conducts training and offers education to reduce risks of accidents at sea. Most of its personnel are volunteers, and it depends largely on contributions from the public.

Finally, the path winds its way through a forest to reach **Ploumanac'h** (**2hr 30min**). You arrive at **Plage de Saint-Guirec**, with an oratory dedicated to that saint standing between the low- and high-tide lines. Walk across this beach and climb steps leading to a trail among large rocks. The trail soon enters a forest, heading west and then turning south.

Emerging from the forest, descend on Chemin de la Pointe. Walk along Quai Bellevue beside Ploumanac'h's harbour. Turn right to cross a dyke at the end of the quay. In the middle of the dyke there is an old tidal mill (*moulin à marée*). Turn right after the dyke and walk along the beach (or a path beside it at high tide) to reach a road. Follow that road across another dyke with a second tidal mill. ▶

This mill, built in 1764, was used principally to grind grain, but also to process flax for the production of linen and to crush salt.

At the end of the dyke, turn right to continue walking around the perimeter of the harbour. Walk through a parking lot and follow a narrow lane. Turn left where the lane broadens and walk to an intersection. Turn sharply right on a smaller, gravel road, Chemin de Costaeres. This road leads to **Plage de Tourony** (**3hr 15min**). Turn left to walk beside this beach and left on a path among trees. Pass a field with picnic tables and walk beside another beach.

After going around a promontory (nearly 1km from Plage de Tourony), turn right to walk on a dirt path atop a stone dyke. Turn right after 250 metres to walk through a gap in the dyke onto a beach. ◀ Walk 500 metres on the beach and leave it on steps leading to Quai de Sainte Anne. Turn right immediately on Boulevard du Coz Pors and continue north beside the beach.

At high tide, turn left (south) here and right on a road to reach Quai de Sainte Anne.

Turn right on a pedestrian path just beyond Allée des Goélands. (The GR34 follows a scenic route from here to Coz Pors, but, if you prefer, you can walk directly there by continuing on Boulevard du Coz Pors.) Turn left on a path beside the water and pass a parking area. The GR34 continues straight on a sandy path to **Coz Pors en Trégastel**.

These granite boulders appear ready to tumble into the sea

STAGE 21

Trégastel (Coz Pors) to Île Grande

Start	Trégastel (Coz Pors)
Finish	Île Grande
Distance	15.5km +7km around Île Grande
Ascent	190m +65m on Île Grande
Descent	195m +65m on Île Grande
Time	4hr +1hr 45min around Île Grande
Map	IGN TOP25 0714OT
Refreshments	Cafés/restaurants in Grève Blanche, Landrellec, Penvern, Île Grande
Transport	TILT line D
Accommodation	*Chambres d'hôtes* in Penvern, Île Grande; campgrounds in Landrellec, Île Grande

This stage offers an easy walk, without strenuous climbs or descents. There is interesting variety: spectacular pink granite boulders; a broad, sandy beach; quiet forests; open coastal moorland; and finally Île Grande, which is scarcely an island at low tide but definitely seems detached from the mainland.

This stage begins in **Coz Pors** where Boulevard du Coz Pors and Rue du Générale de Gaulle meet, facing a beach. Offshore, the extraordinary cubical rock, Le Dé (the Die), captures the eye. Turn left (southwest); walk past restaurants and bathing cabins. Descend steps and follow a trail around a promontory amid great boulders. A left turn reveals **Grève Blanche**, a broad beach with bathing cabins that are, of course, painted white.

Continue on the trail, climbing a rock above Grève Blanche. Descend from here, turn right toward the beach and left to walk on the embankment. At the end of the embankment, turn left on a sandy path and continue on Rue des 3 Grèves. At the end of this road, follow a path to the left toward a prominent hill.

The trail forks at the base of the hill; the left fork is the best route over the top. Descend on the right side of this hill and walk on a trail beside Plage de Toull Bihan. The trail continues after the beach, first enclosed by bushes, then in a pine forest – a pleasant, easy walk.

The trail emerges from the forest at a small road beside **Baie de Kerlavos**. Continue straight (west) on a surfaced road. The road leads to a trail through a forest, then returns to the water's edge. Walk over large rocks to a beach. Continue on a dirt road between two houses to an open space surrounded by more houses.

Turn right here on a delightful trail, first through a pine forest beside the bay then in open country along the coast. After a short walk on a road, pass Landrellec's **campground** and a restaurant close to the beach (**1hr 20min**). Offshore, clusters of rocks emerge from the water. The trail curves left past an anchorage for pleasure craft, and the white dome of the Cité des Télécoms rises above the trees in the distance. ◀ Walk through another **campground** and cross a stream on a small bridge.

The GR34 turns inland to approach **Landrellec**, but does not enter the town, returning instead to the coast (**2hr**). Follow the trail (which becomes a dirt road) to a main road. Turn right to walk 100 metres along a path

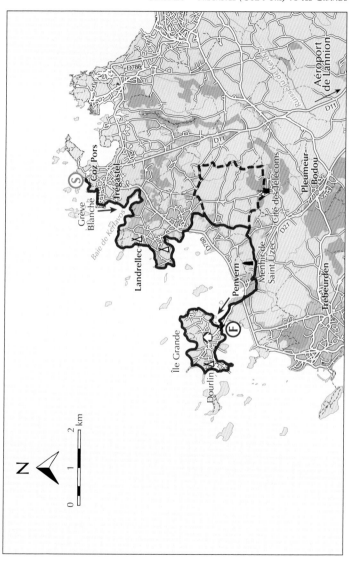

parallel to the road, then cross the road and follow a dirt road that branches to the right. Follow this road into a residential area and turn right on Route du Brouster. A T-junction offers a choice: the official route of the GR34, indicated by a sign, turns left here for a long ramble through the countryside. Another sign shows an alternative route to the right.

Those who wish to visit the nearby telecommunications museum (www.cite-telecoms.com) should select the official route, which is well marked. However, this route is not particularly attractive and is therefore shown as a variant on the map in this guide. The alternative, described here, is essentially a short-cut: 1.4km from this T-junction to where the two routes meet, compared with 5.8km along the official route. (The overall statistics provided in the stage information box are based on the following alternative route.)

The alternative route is marked with yellow blazes. Turn right at the T-junction. Walk through a residential neighbourhood, cross a road and continue straight on a forest trail. Follow a road after the trail emerges from the forest, cross a road and walk on Chemin du Clos-Moulong. After 600 metres you reach a surfaced path. The GR34 arrives here from the left; turn right to rejoin it (**2hr 45min**).

The Menhir de Saint Uzec was erected between 5000 and 4000 BCE and 'Christianised' in the 17th century: carved with religious imagery and surmounted by a cross.

The path enters the woods and is no longer surfaced. Turn left on a trail and continue straight through an intersection. A further 700 metres brings you to an unusual **menhir**. ◄ Turn right on a road and descend to Route de l'Île Grande. Turn left and then right on a small road, which becomes Rue de Keralegan before passing Penvern chapel (originally built around 1300). Turn right after the chapel to reach a T-junction with a main road (**3hr 30min**).

Turn left and immediately right at a fork to follow another road toward Île Grande. This is a busy road; you will be pleased to branch right on Allée de Crec'han Tantadou. Descend to a path on a beach. A trail to the left soon leaves the beach, going toward

Trébeurden. ▶ Continue straight for Île Grande and curve left at the end of the beach to reach a **bridge** to the island.

To reach the commercial centre of Île Grande, continue straight after the bridge. However, the GR34 circles the island: turn right after the bridge and walk to a T-junction. Turn right and walk into the dunes and wetlands along a well-maintained trail. Pass a sailing centre. From here, the trail follows the coast. About 2.5km from the bridge, there is a memorial to the stone masons who once worked here: Tréguier's cathedral was built with granite from Île Grande. Further on, the trail passes Station LPO, an ornithological centre.

> The Ligue pour la Protection des Oiseaux (League for the Protection of Birds) cares for birds that have been harmed by pollution and other human activities. It manages the **Sept Îles bird sanctuary**. A sign here reminds visitors not to feed convalescent birds in a large outdoor enclosure.

On the west side of the island, the trail passes a restaurant and a **campground**. Walk past the Saint-Saveur anchorage and conclude the circuit of Île Grande by turning left in front of houses that face the mainland and continuing back to the **bridge**.

You will return to this point at the beginning of the next stage.

Île Grande

STAGE 22
Île Grande to Le Yaudet

Start	Île Grande
Finish	Le Yaudet
Distance	30.5km
Ascent	850m
Descent	810m
Time	9hr
Map	IGN TOP25 0714OT
Refreshments	Cafés/restaurants in Trébeurden, Beg Léguer, Lannion, Le Yaudet
Transport	TILT lines D, 30; BreizhGo line 27; railway service in Lannion
Accommodation	Hotels and/or *chambres d'hôtes* in Trébeurden, Beg Léguer, Lannion, Le Yaudet

This stage has appealing variety. A walk through fields and forests leads to Trébeurden, where you hike over two rocky promontories: Le Castel and Pointe de Bihit. The GR34 follows the coast in open country after Trébeurden until it reaches the long, narrow Léguer ria. A walk on a tow path up the right bank reaches Lannion; the path beside the left bank passes through a forest to Le Yaudet.

A short side-trail off the road southeast of this crossing leads to the Pajou Menhir (third millennium BCE).

If you spent the night on **Île Grande**, begin this stage by crossing the bridge; then turn left on a path to the beach. Walk 350 metres along the beach and turn right on a path, following a sign that points to Trébeurden. Cross the road and continue in the same direction across a field. ◄

After 800 metres, cross a road and continue along a small, surfaced road. Make a dogleg right/left turn onto Chemin de Leur Huelan. The road climbs gently, becoming a pleasant forest trail. At a fork, bear right toward Trébeurden Port. The trail descends gradually, then climbs again to leave the forest (**45min**).

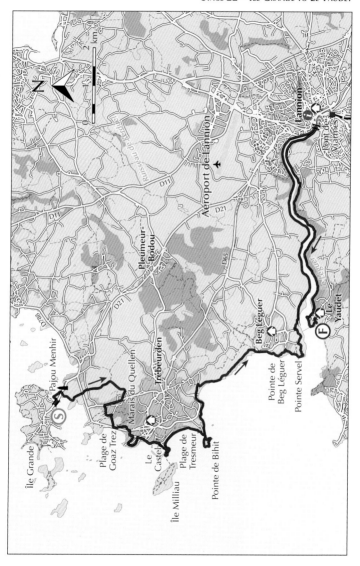

The GR34 now winds its way through Trébeurden. Turn right on a road in a residential area, right again at an intersection with Rue de Kerariou, and left on Chemin de Rougoulouarn. Where this road curves right, follow a small road steeply downhill to the left. Make a hairpin right turn on Chemin de Crec'h Hellen and continue downhill to **Plage de Goas Treiz**.

Turn left to walk beside the main road and left after 100 metres on Rue de Quellen. Pass a park, **Marais du Quellen**, and walk through a neighbourhood of attractive homes. Cross a road on a left/right dogleg and continue on Rue de Kerellec.

'Père Trébeurden' on Le Castel

The GR34 now tours this neighbourhood: turn right on Rue de Roc'h Ascoat and left on Allée Circulaire de Lan Kerellec, which leads back to Rue de Kerellec. Descend Rue de Pors-Termen to Trébeurden's harbour, passing a monument dedicated to Aristide Briand. ▸

Walk along the quay past restaurants (**2hr**). At the end of the quay, follow a path around **Le Castel**, which looms over the harbour. It's a lovely trail among trees and extraordinary boulders – in particular, 'Père Trébeurden'. The trail passes **Île Milliau**, accessible at low tide.

The path around Le Castel returns to its starting point. Walk from here on the embankment beside the long, graceful curve of **Plage de Tresmeur**, where there are additional restaurants. At the end of the embankment, continue on a trail that climbs a hill overlooking the beach. At a fork in this trail, descend steps carved in rock.

Pass between two stone pillars and walk a short distance on a surfaced road toward two houses. The path around **Pointe de Bihit** begins and ends here. There are some steep bits and rocks to scramble over, but it's worth the effort; there are great views in all directions.

Briand (1862–1932), a leading politician of the Third Republic and Nobel Prize laureate, spent holidays with his companion, Lucie Jourdan, in her home on Île Milliau.

Clouds over Île Milliau and Le Castel

WALKING THE BRITTANY COAST PATH

On completing the loop around Pointe de Bihit (**2hr 45min**), follow the trail that veers right just before the two stone pillars and walk behind the white-and-blue house that you admired from afar. The trail traverses a slope for 1km, leading to a road (gravel at first, then surfaced). The GR34 soon turns right onto a trail.

Cross a road, continue straight for 300 metres and turn right on a road down to a trail in open country beside the coast. Bear right (direction: Falaises de Beg Léguer) at a fork in the trail that is poorly marked. You soon reach Plage de Goas Lagorn, 3.7km from Pointe de Bihit (**4hr**).

Continue straight after a parking area, passing a café/restaurant. The trail passes **Pointe de Beg Léguer** and curves left around **Pointe Servel**. The GR34 follows the right bank of the Léguer ria from here to Lannion. After passing a small parking area, the trail descends in the forest to a road. Turn left to walk close to the water; then take a right fork that leads to an old tow path.

The path follows the curves of the river for more than 4km, leading to Quai de la Corderie, which becomes Quai du Maréchal Joffre. Walk 500 metres along these quays to a roundabout beside a bridge, **Pont de Viarmes** (**7hr**). Leave the roundabout to the left to reach the centre of **Lannion**.

Lannion grew in the Middle Ages around a ford that was the closest point to the coast where the Léguer could be crossed at high tide. Half-timbered buildings from the 15–16th centuries have survived in the centre. Lannion became a centre for research and technology with the establishment in the 1960s of the Centre National d'Études des Télécommunications (CNET). Some telecom companies that were attracted to the area by the presence of the CNET have struggled in recent years to adapt to competition and technological change. Lannion is now part of a *pôle de compétitivité* called Images et Réseaux (Media and Networks competitive cluster).

The GR34 returns to the coast along the left bank: cross the bridge and turn right to walk beside the river on a gravel path. The path ends 2km from the bridge in a parking lot. Walk up steps beside a small fountain at the far end of the parking lot. A short climb leads to a delightful trail in the woods.

At a point where a trail branches left toward a windmill (3.5km after entering the woods), continue straight and then, 1km further on, turn left. The trail reaches a vantage point, where there is an old customs hut. Continue around the headland, passing another lookout building, and turn left to climb steps leading to **Le Yaudet**. Turn left off the GR34 beside the chapel to walk into this village, which has a pleasant *chambres d'hôtes* and restaurant.

LE YAUDET

Le Yaudet, commanding the entrance to the estuary, was already a fortified place when the Romans arrived. (*The Independent* reported in its issue dated 1 April 1993 that archaeologists had found ruins of Astérix's home village at Le Yaudet.) The Gallo-Roman village thrived from farming and maritime commerce, but suffered during ninth-century Viking raids. Le Yaudet's chapel was built in 1860 on the site of earlier edifices: a Roman temple and a medieval chapel. Nolwenn Leroy, a popular Breton singer, recorded a video of her song 'Juste pour me souvenir' ('Just to remember') in this chapel: walking among ex-voto models of ships hanging from the ceiling, she remembers *'ce dernier baiser amer'* ('that bitter last kiss') and wonders whether she can ever forgive the sea that took her lover away…

STAGE 23
Le Yaudet to Locquirec

Start	Le Yaudet
Finish	Locquirec (Place du Port)
Distance	27km
Ascent	825m
Descent	860m
Time	8hr
Maps	IGN TOP25 0714OT, 0615ET
Refreshments	Cafés/restaurants in Locquémeau, Saint-Michel-en-Grève, Saint-Efflam, Plestin-les-Grèves (Quai de Toul an Héry), Locquirec
Transport	TILT line 30
Accommodation	Hotels and/or *chambres d'hôtes* in Locquémeau, Kermorvan, Plestin-les-Grèves, Locquirec; campground in Locquirec

This is a memorable stage. It begins with a trail close to the water. Then, between Locquémeau and Saint-Michel-en-Grève, the GR34 traverses steep slopes high above the rocky shore. It's quite dramatic. One short section is exposed but can be avoided by following a variant. After the Beg Douar headland, the route stays close to the water again for an easy approach to Locquirec.

At low tide, a line of rocks across the Baie de la Vierge is visible. This structure was probably built during the sixth–seventh centuries as part of a tidal mill.

Walk southwest from **Le Yaudet**'s chapel and continue through a clearing (Roche Plate) with a great view over the bay. The trail curves left and descends in a forest. On reaching a road, turn right and enter **Pont-Rous**. Cross a bridge and turn right on a road that climbs gradually among houses. Fork right on a gravel road that descends to the coast. ◀

The trail follows the coast, generally west and level, for 1.3km and then enters a forest. Continue straight where another trail branches left. A signpost points to

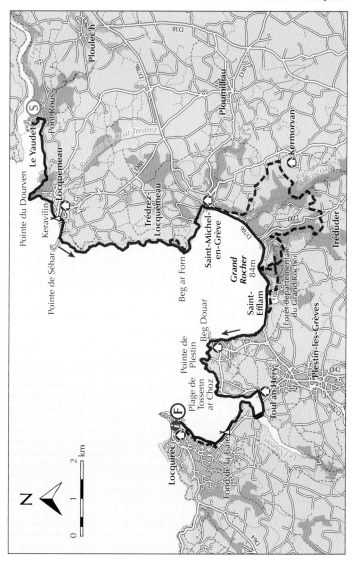

Locquémeau and Saint-Michel-en-Grève: this trail is generally well marked, so watch for GR marks that show the way and others (X) that indicate the wrong direction. Pass a beautiful little beach (Saint-Quiriou) and fork right to continue beside the water.

The trail goes around **Pointe du Dourven**, close to the rocky shore. Descend on a gravel road to Plage de Notigou and enter **Locquémeau** on a surfaced road. Turn right on Corniche de Notigou and right again on Rue du Port. This road leads to **Pointe de Séhar**, where there is a café and a restaurant, but the GR34 turns left on a gravel road before reaching those buildings (**1hr 30min**).

After a narrow passage through bushes and ferns, the trail emerges in the open and follows the coast.

About 4km after Locquémeau, a sign points to St-Michel-en-Grève and warns that the way ahead is steep ('*PRUDENCE PASSAGES ESCARPÉS!*'). Indeed, the trail goes up and down as it crosses a steep slope, and the path itself is narrow. If you are not comfortable on such a trail, you can avoid this section by following an obvious signed path that branches left here and rejoins the GR34 at Beg ar Forn.

The exposed trail across Beg ar Forn

The trail goes around a headland, **Beg ar Forn**, and – as you would expect on a trail across a steep slope above a rocky coastline – the views are breathtaking. Once past the exposed section, the trail drops down to **Saint-Michel-en-Grève** (**3hr 45min**).

As you pause, perhaps, for refreshment at a café here, you can choose among three ways of walking to Saint-Efflam.

The official GR34

The official GR34 follows a long inland route to Saint-Efflam (12km). It's a good trail with GR marks (and accommodation near Kermovan), but you may prefer a shorter route if you're walking from Le Yaudet all the way to Locquirec. The longer route is shown as a variant on the map.

At low tide, walk southwest across the vast beach (3km). Your goal, Saint-Efflam, is a cluster of buildings to the right of Grand Rocher, a prominent hill. There may be shallow pools or streams of water along the way.

At high tide, water can fill the beach right up to the sea wall. In that case, walk a short distance in the dunes near Saint-Michel-en-Grève and then continue on pavement beside the road to a point after **Grand Rocher** where you can return to the dunes in the approach to **Saint-Efflam** (4km). This direct approach is the main route on the map.

Walk from Saint-Efflam beside the main road, then fork right in a cul-de-sac and pass a park. Follow a trail to the left into the woods. After a short climb up steps, the trail levels off, leading to a road. Continue straight and return to the woods on a pleasant trail to the parking area for **Beg Douar**, 2.5km from Saint-Efflam (**5hr 30min**).

Follow the trail to the left of the parking area. Pass Porz Mellec – an inviting, secluded beach. Turn left on a road above the beach and then right. Continue straight on a trail into the forest where the road curves left. ▶ Walk along this trail to a fork: turn right and walk up steps to **Pointe de Plestin** with views across the bay to Locquirec.

If submerged at high tide, the trail ahead can be avoided by continuing on the road.

157

A hidden gem: Plage de Porz Mellec

Turn right at a trail T-junction to continue on the coast around the bay. Walk down steps carved in the rock facing **Plage de Tossenn ar Choz** and up a ramp that leads to a parking area. Turn right on a road, then right again. This road curves left above a beach. Bear left on a trail before the road descends to a parking area. The trail passes the ruins of the Roman Hogolo baths. A path beside the water leads to a road in **Toul an Héry**: turn right here and pass a *crêperie* and a *chambres d'hôtes* (**7hr**).

The department's name is derived from the Latin *finis terrae* – thus analogous to Lands' End in England.

Crossing the **bridge** ahead, you enter the Department of Finistère. ◀ Turn right after the bridge on a trail and then right on a road. Walk a short distance on this road, then veer right on a trail beside the water in a protected area, La Dune de l'Île Blanche. Follow a left fork, cross a road and continue straight on a trail into the woods. The trail leads to a road: turn right beside a **campground** and then left on a path between the campground and a beach.

The high-tide route, which climbs from the beach here, has standard GR marks and is shown as a variant on the map.

Continue past the campground on a trail marked as a low-tide 'diversion' on the beach. ◀ After a walk on the rocky beach, go up a ramp beside a storage area for dinghies. Proceed on the embankment, passing a sailing school, to arrive in **Locquirec**'s Place du Port.

STAGE 24
Locquirec to Plougasnou

Start	Locquirec
Finish	Plougasnou (Place Général Leclerc)
Distance	20km (18.5km for the inland variant)
Ascent	910m (490m for the inland variant)
Descent	840m (440m for the inland variant)
Time	6hr (5hr 15min for inland variant)
Map	IGN TOP25 0615ET
Refreshments	Cafés/restaurants at Moulin de la Rive, Poul Rodou, Plougasnou
Transport	TILT line 30; Linéotim line 20
Accommodation	Campground in Saint-Jean-du-Doigt; a *chambres d'hôtes* in Plougasnou

This stage follows the coast with considerable variety. The first part is a placid trail close to the water, passing attractive little beaches. The latter part remains close to the water, but the terrain is dramatic: the trail climbs and descends steep slopes. The trail itself is not technically difficult, but it's a physical workout. (An inland variant offers an easier route.) The scenery is spectacular!

Walk from **Locquirec**'s Place du Port northeast on Rue de l'Église, passing a church, a war memorial and a building with striking trompe-l'œil paintings. The road leads to a coastal path around **Pointe de Locquirec** to Plage de Porz Biliec. Pass a boat ramp and turn right on a road to follow the curve of the beach.

Leave the road just before it curves left to walk on a trail to the right above the beach. Turn left on a road beside an old *lavoir* and immediately right on a trail. Turn right at the next road, then left on a trail at the end of the road.

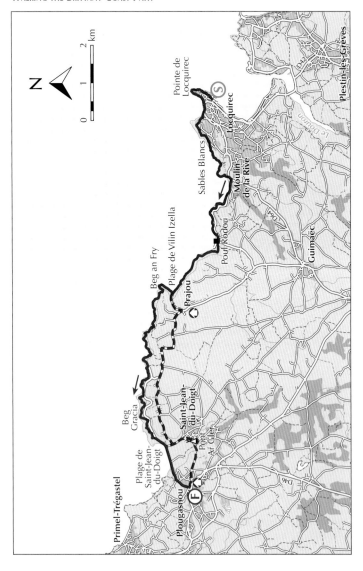

Primel-Trégastel

Plage de Saint-Jean-du-Doigt

Plougasnou

Beg Gracia

Saint-Jean-du-Doigt

Pont ar Cter

Beg an Fry

Plage de Vilin Izella

Prajou

Pont/Rodou

Sables Blancs

Moulin de la Rive

Pointe de Locquirec

Locquirec

Le Douron

Guimaëc

Plestin-les-Grèves

N

km

Further along the coast, you can pause at a bench above **Sables Blancs** and admire the view. Then walk across the grass between the beach and a road to pick up the GR34, which starts as a surfaced road and soon becomes a trail. Walk a short distance beside a road and turn right on a smaller road (direction: Saint-Jean-du-Doigt). After 400 metres, turn right on a rocky trail that climbs and descends beside the coast.

Follow this trail for nearly 2km to the beach at **Moulin de la Rive** (**1hr 15min**). Turn right on the road behind the beach, then right again after a short distance. Follow the trail that soon branches right. The trail leads to **Poul Rodou**, where there is a well-known café/bookstore, CapLan & Co.

Continue on a forest trail beside the coast for 2.5km to the parking area for **Plage de Vilin Izella**. A side-trail leaves the GR34 here and takes an inland route to Saint-Jean-du-Doigt, thus avoiding the strenuous coastal stretch.

Inland variant
From the Plage de Vilin Izella parking area, follow the side-trail for the easier inland variant (all tarmac). Walk past the Moulin de Trobodec, a restored watermill with an unusually large wheel, to a small village, **Prajou** (600 metres). Turn right at an intersection and walk 2.8km on this road to a fork. Bear right here and turn right after 700 metres at a T-junction. Descend after 1km to Route de la Plage: turn right to rejoin the GR34 (300 metres) and then left towards Plougasnou as described below, or turn left for Saint-Jean-du-Doigt.

The GR34 turns right toward the beach and passes a memorial commemorating actions of the French Resistance and the Royal Navy (**2hr 30min**). The hike from here is arduous – 6km of climbs and descents on a trail that is often rocky (but equipped with steps in places). If you're ready for such a hike, you will enjoy it. The views over the water and along the coast are, of course, spectacular.

The GR34 beckons you to adventure between Beg an Fry and Beg Gracia

The trail climbs first from Plage de Vilin Izella to **Beg an Fry**, 80m above sea level. Enjoy the view while it lasts, as the trail promptly descends from this high point. There are several climbs and descents after this, along with sweeping traverses across the steep slope. After several kilometres of this walking, you are almost startled when the trail levels off beside a road (**5hr 30min**). Enjoy a rest on the bench here and soak in the view over **Plage de Saint-Jean-du-Doigt**.

The inland variant rejoins the GR34 here.

Turn right on the road and walk to the beach. Route de la Plage forms an 'L' here: left to Saint-Jean-du-Doigt (1km away); straight to Plougasnou. ◄

Lower Brittany is famous for its **enclos paroissiaux** (parish closes), which comprise a triumphal arch in a wall enclosing a Calvary, ossuary and cemetery beside a church. Lavishly carved and decorated, the *enclos paroissiaux* reflect the prosperity and piety (plus local rivalries) of Brittany during the 15–17th centuries. Saint-Jean-du-Doigt's *enclos paroissial* is a good exemplar of these ornate structures. The town is named for a relic that it acquired in the 15th century: a bone from the index finger of Saint John the Baptist. A reliquary containing this bone is displayed in the church's treasury.

If you make a detour to visit Saint-Jean-du-Doigt and then wish to go to Plougasnou, you need not backtrack to the main road: a path (shown on the map) leads from Saint-Jean-du-Doigt to Plougasnou. Turn left in the woods after 200 metres on this path.

The GR34 follows Route de la Plage toward **Plougasnou** but does not enter the town's centre: 1km from the beach, it makes a hairpin right turn on Chemin de Lézouzard, passing the Ker Maria oratory on the right. To reach the centre, do not make this turn but instead walk 400 metres further to Place Général Leclerc.

The GR34 traces a dramatic route above the cliffs between Beg an Fry and Beg Gracia

STAGE 25
Plougasnou to Saint-Samson

Start	Plougasnou
Finish	Saint-Samson
Distance	13.5km
Ascent	300m
Descent	370m
Time	3hr 45min
Map	IGN TOP25 0615ET
Refreshments	Cafés/restaurants in Primel-Trégastel, Le Diben, Saint-Samson
Transport	Linéotim line 20
Accommodation	Hotels and/or *chambres d'hôtes* in Primel-Trégastel, Le Diben; *gîte d'étape* in Saint-Samson

The middle section of this stage includes a significant amount of urban walking (with the advantage that there are cafés/restaurants). Balancing those kilometres on tarmac, the earlier and latter sections are outstanding coastal paths. The trail stays close to the water and its rocky coast. You can touch those awesome boulders!

To rejoin the GR34 from the centre of **Plougasnou**, walk back on Route de la Plage. Fork left on Chemin de Lezouzard and turn right on a gravel path that leads to the coastal trail. It's an easy walk close to the rocky shore.

After 2.5km on the coastal trail, you reach a beach in **Primel-Trégastel**. Walk on the pavement beside the beach, passing a restaurant and *chambres d'hôtes*. At the end of the beach, turn left on Rue du Grand Large, then right on Rue de Karreg an Ty. Pass a campground and walk around rocky **Pointe de Primel (1hr 15min)**, crowned by its *cabane du douanier* (customs officer's cabin).

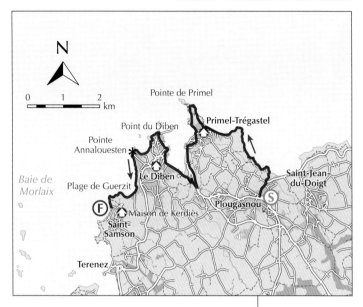

Turn right at a T-junction on Rue de Rhun Predou and then left on Rue de Kereven. Cross a road, continue straight on Chemin de Parc ar Born and (through an intersection) Chemin de la Carrière, leading to a grass path among houses. Turn left at a parking lot to walk on a path beside a road, leading to Chemin de Bellevue.

Walk along Chemin de Bellevue for 800 metres and turn right to cross a road. Descend Chemin de Tromelin, with the bay in sight ahead. Follow this road through a hairpin left turn and a right turn; then turn right on a small road. Turn left at a T-junction to walk past a shipyard.

Turn right after 800 metres on a narrow path. Turn left at water's edge to walk back up a small road (Impasse du Quinquai). Continue straight on Venelle de Perros to a T-junction, and turn right to walk through an industrial area. Turn left to cross a road and follow a trail beside a beach, then a road among houses. This road reaches a T-junction with Rue du Port: turn right here

The GR34 stays close to the coast between Pointe du Diben and Pointe Annalouesten

and immediately left on a trail at **Pointe du Diben** (**2hr 30min**).

After 4km of this urban meandering, the GR34 now rewards your patience with one of its finest coastal trails. The path does not carve a route high above the sea; instead it stays low, giving you a close look at extraordinary boulders. Everybody likes fine, sunny weather, but (wearing the right clothes, of course) you can also appreciate the drama of a good storm producing waves that crash over these rocks, sending plumes of spray in all directions.

The trail follows the curve of Plage du Port Blanc and goes over **Pointe Annalouesten**, with broad views over the Baie de Morlaix. Descend a steep slope on the west side of this headland. Follow a trail through bushes and woods, past houses, to trace an arc around **Plage de Guerzit** (**3hr 15min**). A sign warns against collecting pebbles (*galets*): taking them is theft (*'un vol'*).

Return to the coastal trail and continue around a small headland (Pointe de Perhérel). The GR34 reaches **Saint-Samson**'s beach, where a sign points the way uphill to Maison de Kerdiès, a comfortable *gîte d'étape* with a good restaurant.

STAGE 26
Saint-Samson to Morlaix

Start	Saint-Samson
Finish	Morlaix (Place Charles de Gaulle)
Distance	21km
Ascent	365m
Descent	365m
Time	5hr
Map	IGN TOP25 0615ET
Refreshments	Cafés/restaurants in Térénez, Dourduff-en-Mer, Ploujean, Morlaix
Transport	Linéotim line 20; railway service in Morlaix
Accommodation	A *chambres d'hôtes* in Térénez; hotels, *chambres d'hôtes*, youth hostel in Morlaix

This stage leaves behind the spectacular coastal scenery of cliffs, boulders and crashing waves. It's an easy walk around the little Anse de Térénez and beside the Rade de Morlaix. The highlights of the stage are the Barnénez Cairn and the destination: Morlaix, a lively and interesting city.

Depart from **Saint-Samson**'s beach: walk on a grassy bluff above the beach and go around a large apartment building. Back on the coastal trail, walk around a headland buttressed by large rocks. Continue straight after a beach to reach **Térénez**.

Walk on the road past a restaurant and turn left. The road rises gently beside a small oyster facility. Turn right to descend to the water's edge and pass an old *lavoir*. The trail cuts through large bushes and ferns, offering occasional glimpses of the water.

You reach a road at the head of this small bay, **Anse de Térénez**. Turn right to cross a stream on a bridge and right again on a trail back into the woods. The path runs beside the road, continuing straight when the road curves left.

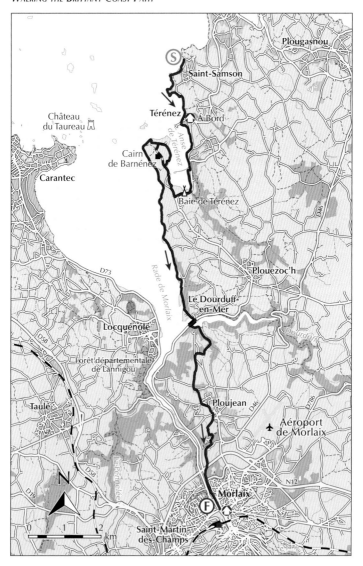

Turn right at a T-junction and, 200 metres further, right on a small road toward the water (**1hr 45min**). Walk beside the bay for 300 metres and turn left on a small road that merges into Route de Barnénez. The GR34 turns right on a gravel road, where a sign points to 'Petite Grève', to go around the Barnénez peninsula; however, it is worth continuing straight here to visit the **Barnénez Cairn**, just 150 metres further up the road. If you do so, continue on Route de Barnénez beyond the Cairn to rejoin the GR34.

BARNÉNEZ CAIRN

The great Cairn de Barnénez

Barnénez Cairn was discovered by chance – and nearly destroyed in the process. A contractor obtained permission from the landowner to use two rocky mounds as a quarry for the construction of a road. He had cleared one of those mounds and begun to dig into the second when, in May 1955, a journalist discovered what he was doing, understood its significance and sounded the alarm. The authorities quickly stopped the quarrying. Excavations uncovered an extraordinary cairn – Europe's largest – that had been constructed in the fifth millennium BCE. It is about 60 metres long, 28 metres wide and 9 metres high. A cross-section revealing techniques used to build the cairn is visible, thanks – ironically – to the removal of stone from that sector by the contractor.

To follow the GR34 from the right turn off Route de Barnénez, continue straight to the water's edge and turn

Dourduff-en-Mer

This is where you rejoin the GR34 if walking from the Cairn de Barnénez.

left on a trail that goes around Pointe de Barnénez. After 600 metres on this trail, turn left on a road and immediately right on a trail that continues in the woods (**2hr 30min**). ◄ Walk beside the water, passing an old *lavoir* and a grove of pine trees. Offshore, the Château du Taureau stands vigil.

The trail emerges from the woods. Walk past a group of homes and an oyster facility, and continue on a road for a short distance. Where the road curves left, follow a trail straight into the woods. The trail joins a road that leads to **Le Dourduff-en-Mer**, an attractive village. Turn left to walk along the row of houses facing the harbour, then right to cross a **bridge** over the Dourduff River (**4hr**).

The GR34 now turns inland to approach Morlaix: turn left after the bridge to walk along a path in the woods beside the river. Turn right on a road and, after 50 metres, right on a trail that passes an agricultural high school (*lycée agricole*). Follow a right fork, cross a road and continue straight on Rue de Pors Land. Turn right in a small cul-de-sac after this road curves left. Walk briefly on a trail, then continue on a surfaced road. Turn left at a T-junction on Rue des Perdrix.

Cross Rue de la Maison de Paille on the western side of **Ploujean** and walk along a tree-lined dirt road. A sign points left for a pedestrian path to Morlaix; the

GR34 continues straight here but will join this path shortly. Curve left and turn right/left through a group of farm buildings. Finally, 100 metres after passing the farm buildings, turn left on the path marked for Morlaix and follow a trail in the woods. Pause to observe the interior of a large, cylindrical structure: a dovecot.

Leave the forest through a gate and continue on a road. You soon pass under a towering motorway viaduct. ▶ Turn left after the viaduct on a road and walk beside the river through a commercial area and port into Morlaix. The GR34 turns right to cross a bridge and follow the left bank of the river back to the coast. However, continue straight without crossing the bridge through Place Charles de Gaulle for the centre of **Morlaix**.

The railway viaduct that is Morlaix's famous landmark – 58 metres high, 292 metres long, completed in 1864 – straddles the city 1.5km from here.

MORLAIX

Morlaix prospered in the 15–18th centuries as an entrepôt for trade in linen as well as salt, leather, lead and wine. The town was thus an attractive target for an English seaborne force that captured and sacked Morlaix in 1522. The English fleet was commanded by Admiral Thomas Howard, later 3rd Duke of Norfolk (uncle of Anne Boleyn and Katherine Howard, the two wives of Henry VIII who were beheaded). His flagship was the *Mary Rose*, a famous warship that later sank in a battle against the French in the Solent. (The *Mary Rose* was discovered in 1971, raised in 1982 and preserved; it can now be

Morlaix, with its famous railway viaduct in the background

visited in Portsmouth.) Accounts differ as to what happened next: as Bretons tell the story, the English attackers who remained after the withdrawal of the main force drank a lot of the wine that they found in the town, so they were not ready for the vigorous counterattack the next day that routed them. At any rate, the Morlaisiens had the final word, as they added a punning motto to their coat of arms: *'S'ils te mordent, mords-les'* ('If they bite you, bite them' – *'mords-les'* and 'Morlaix' are homophones).

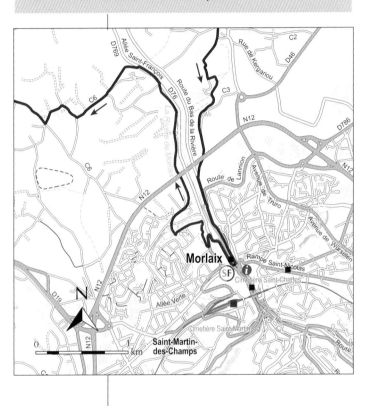

STAGE 27
Morlaix to Carantec

Start	Morlaix
Finish	Carantec (Place de la Libération)
Distance	22.5km (via direct route to centre)
Ascent	605m
Descent	570m
Time	5hr 45min
Map	IGN TOP25 0615ET
Refreshments	Cafés/restaurants in Locquénolé, Carantec
Transport	Linéotim line 28
Accommodation	*Chambres d'hôtes* in Locquénolé; hotels, *chambres d'hôtes* in Carantec

The GR34 returns to the sea in this stage, although you would hardly imagine it during the first half of the walk as the trail meanders in forests, climbing and descending hilly terrain. You move into the open, with views over the Rade de Morlaix after Locquénolé, finishing with a walk on a beach to approach Carantec.

In the centre of **Morlaix**, walk from Place Charles de Gaulle to rejoin the GR34 at the bridge. Cross to the left bank of the river and turn right to walk along the quay.

> The building on the left, **La Manufacture** (1740), was a factory for tobacco products. The building has been converted to other activities – cultural, commercial, educational – since the cessation of tobacco manufacture here in the early 2000s.

On reaching a roundabout, turn left and walk up the road past a youth hostel. Turn right 100 metres after the hostel to pass through an opening in a wall and climb a short flight of steps into the woods. Turn right on a path that climbs steeply but soon levels off. The GR34 turns right where a trail for the Vallée de la Pennélé goes straight. Cross a bridge, walk past apartment buildings and pick up another forest trail straight ahead. Pass under the motorway viaduct on a path that is broad, straight and level.

The trail drops to a road 1km after the viaduct. Walk beside the road, passing a *maison de retraite* (retirement home) and the **Communauté des Augustines** (a monastery). Turn left and walk up a path beside a wall toward the Sanctuaire de la Salette. The path is steep, but bas-reliefs on the wall depicting Stations of the Cross encourage you. The path levels off in open country and continues on a surfaced road (**1hr**).

The road curves between farm buildings and a beautiful stone house and passes among warehouses and silos devoted to large-scale farming. Turn right after these buildings on a dirt road that becomes a rocky trail descending in a forest. Cross a stream and make a hairpin left turn to walk uphill. Turn right 900 metres after the bridge, walk up a sunken trail and continue in the open on a level trail (**2hr**).

Turn left on a small road and walk past greenhouses. Make a dogleg right/left turn across a road and continue to a fork. Bear right here toward Lavallot and left after 150 metres on a tree-lined path. Leave the trees behind and turn right on a path that crosses open fields. On reaching a road, turn right and, after a short walk, left on a grass path. This path enters a forest and descends to a road. Turn right toward Locquénolé, then right on a trail that climbs.

Over the next 1.5km the trail and its many turns are well marked. The route goes up and down – at one point descending a narrow ridge on a series of steps and later passing a viewpoint facing Dourduff-en-Mer. A final series of steps leads to a road, where there is a **picnic area** (**2hr 45min**).

Having refreshed yourself here, you're ready to climb again! Pick up the GR34 at the far end of the picnic area and follow it uphill to a level path. Turn right, resume

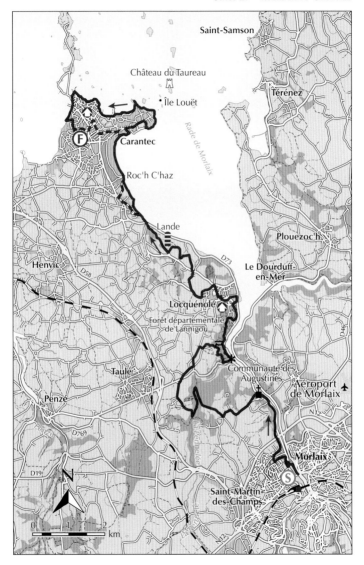

Saint-Samson

Château du Taureau

Île Louët

Térénez

Rade de Morlaix

Carantec

Roc'h C'haz

Lande

Plouezoc'h

Le Dourduff-
en-Mer

Henvic

D58

D73

Locquénolé

Forêt départementale
de Lannigou

D46

Communauté des
Augustines

Aéroport
de Morlaix

Taulé

Penzé

D769

Morlaix

N12

D19

Saint-Martin-
des-Champs

N

0   1   2
km

climbing and turn right on a level path. Follow that path for 150 metres and turn right again to descend on a narrow trail back to the road. A wall blocks access to the road, but that doesn't matter: the GR34 follows the wall to the left a short distance and then climbs back up the hill.

This roller-coaster route finally leaves the forest to enter **Locquénolé**: turn right on a road among houses, right again after 100 metres on a small road and immediately left on a path between a wall and bushes that leads to Rue de Kerliviou. Turn left here, then right on Rue du Clémeur at a T-junction. Follow the road to the river, then

Forest trail between Morlaix and Locquénolé

Open country northwest of Locquénolé

turn left through a park. ▶ The GR34 threads its way through the centre of the village (**3hr 30min**).

> **Locquénolé** is named for Saint Guénolé. The oak tree beside the church was planted during the French Revolution as a liberty tree; it is the only surviving liberty tree in Finistère. (Many liberty trees were cut down after the Restoration in 1814.) The symbolism of such trees may have faded from popular memory, but they remain present in our daily lives: a stylised liberty tree appears on standard French €1 and €2 coins.

Follow a path beside Locquénolé's town hall through a small park and past a *lavoir*. Turn left on Rue du Butou and right around a sports centre on Rue de Prat Santec. Bear left where this road forks and turn left on a grass path that leads to a road: turn right here, left at a T-junction and left on a small road that leads to a narrow trail in the woods. At the end of the trail, turn left to walk to an intersection. Turn right here, left (after 1km) at a T-junction and right onto a road marked as a cul-de-sac.

Continue straight on a path where the tarmac ends. The path enters the woods: turn left on another path beside a bench and a *lavoir*. This path leads after 200 metres to a dirt road; turn right here and right again on a path. A view of the sea opens before you. Walk across the field and into a forest. Turn right at a T-junction with a

▶ You may ignore GR marks that lead across the main road and then back to the park after 100 metres.

If high tide submerges this beach, turn left on the road instead of walking down the steps, and follow a variant with GR marks on roads for 1.3km.

road. The white building on the right, 100 metres after the turn, is the **Lande Lighthouse**.

The GR34 continues straight on a trail in the forest where the road curves left. Turn left onto a road 700 metres after the previous T-junction and walk down to a main road. Cross this road and follow a path beside the water. Walk in front of a large white building (an oyster facility) and pick up the trail behind it. Continue on the coastal path, descending steps to the beach (**4hr 45min**). ◄

Walk on the beach for 1km, pass the parking area at **Roc'h C'haz** (the high-tide variant rejoins the GR34 here) and follow a path between the beach and a golf course. After 1km, you reach another parking area. Where the road forks at the end of this parking area, you have a choice.

If you are planning to spend the night in Carantec, you may wish to take a direct route to the centre of town (1.2km; shown on the map). In that case, fork left on Rue du Clouet and turn left on Rue de Tourville. At a roundabout, turn right on Rue Albert Louppe, which leads to **Place de la Libération** in **Carantec**'s centre.

The GR34 does not enter the centre of Carantec, but rather follows an attractive coastal route around the town, '**Le Tour de Carantec**'. For this option (7km; also shown on the map), fork right from the parking area and walk on a road beside the water. After passing what appear to be derelict oyster facilities, turn left and walk up steps to a road that leads to a roundabout. Turn right here on Rue de Penn al Lann and walk to the **Parc Municipal Claude Goude**. Walk down the terraced slopes of this park. At the exit, turn right and make a hairpin left turn. Walk up to a grove of pine trees and follow a trail with good views over the bay. Offshore, Île Louët, with its lighthouse and cosy white house, looks inviting, in contrast to the grim, stone walls of the Château du Taureau.

The **Château du Taureau** was built in the 1540s to defend Morlaix against attacks from the sea such as the one launched by the English in 1522. The fort

served as a prison in the 18–19th centuries. Auguste Blanqui, the revolutionary socialist, was imprisoned here in 1871. The Château is now open for visits.

Île Louët and Château du Taureau

At **Pointe de Penn al Lann**, the GR34 descends steps to the beach. Walk 300 metres on the beach and climb back to the trail. At a T-junction, turn right to admire the view from **Pointe du Cosmeur** (after which, backtrack to this junction) or turn left to continue. Walk down to Plage du Cosmeur and continue to Plage du Kelenn (cafés/restaurants). At the end of the beach, walk up steps and resume walking around the coast.

The route goes around a promontory, **La Chaise du Curé**, and descends to Plage de la Chaise du Curé. Walk along this beach, then up steps to a narrow walkway leading to **Grève Blanche**. At the end of the beach, walk up a ramp to a parking area. Turn left here and follow a well-marked route through a residential area to Place du Port.

The route returns to a beach beside a jetty. Walk on this beach to a concrete ramp and leave the beach. Walk up **Rue Duguay-Trouin** and turn right on **Rue Jean Bart**. The next stage of the GR34 continues straight where Jean Bart becomes **Rue Guichen** and turns on **Rue Lamotte Piquet** – completing a sequence of streets named after French naval officers who won fame in battles against the British during the 17–18th centuries. To reach the centre of **Carantec**, turn left from Rue Jean Bart on **Rue Kerlizou** and left on **Rue Pasteur** (shown on the map).

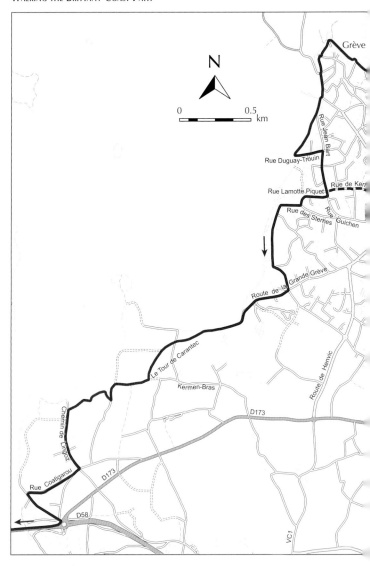

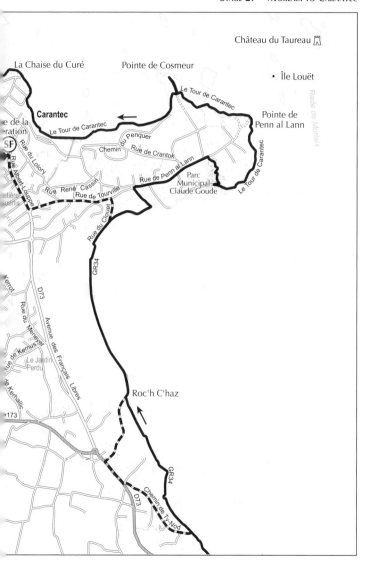

Château du Taureau

La Chaise du Curé

Pointe de Cosmeur

Île Louët

Le Tour de Carantec

Carantec

Pointe de Penn al Lann

e de la ération

Le Tour de Carantec

Rade de Morlaix

SF

Rue du Lolory

Chemin du Penquer

Rue de Crantok

Chemin

Rue René Cassin

Rue Albert-Louppe

Rue de Penn al Lann

Le Tour de Carantec

Rue de Tourville

Parc Municipal Claude Goude

etière aris

Rue du Crouet

GR34

Kerrot

D73

Rue du Menesyer

Avenue des Français Libres

Rue de Kernus

Le Jardin Perdu

Roc'h C'haz

e Kermallic

173

GR34

D73

Chemin de Ti-Nod

STAGE 28
Carantec to Roscoff

Start	Carantec
Finish	Roscoff (Quai d'Auxerre)
Distance	20km
Ascent	290m
Descent	315m
Time	5hr
Map	IGN TOP25 0615ET
Refreshments	Cafés/restaurants in Pempoul, Saint-Pol-de-Léon, Roscoff
Transport	BreizhGo line 29; ferry service in Roscoff; currently no railway service
Accommodation	Hotels, *chambres d'hôtes* in Saint-Pol-de-Léon, Roscoff

If you've been hiking the GR34 from Mont-Saint-Michel, this is a momentous stage: the end of a long trek – unless you intend to continue walking! The GR34 does not, after all, end in Roscoff. The walk from Carantec to Roscoff is easy. The trail circles the bay, staying close to the water, so there are no dramatic cliffs or crashing waves on rocky shores to catch the eye, but there are several attractive beaches along the way. Roscoff is a pleasant place to celebrate your achievement, as it has numerous cafés and restaurants in a scenic setting beside its harbour. You could also visit the attractive Île de Batz, reached by boats from Roscoff.

This route is shown in detail on the Carantec urban map in Stage 27.

In the centre of **Carantec**, walk south from Place de la Libération and turn right on Rue Pasteur, then right on Rue de Kerlizou to a T-junction where you meet the GR34. ◀ Turn left on Rue Guichen and right on Rue Lamotte Piquet. Follow this road as it descends to a shipyard. Walk along Route du Varquez, which curves left into a residential area, and turn right on Route de la Grande Grève.

Walk beside this road to a beach and continue straight on a path beside an artichoke field. Cross a road

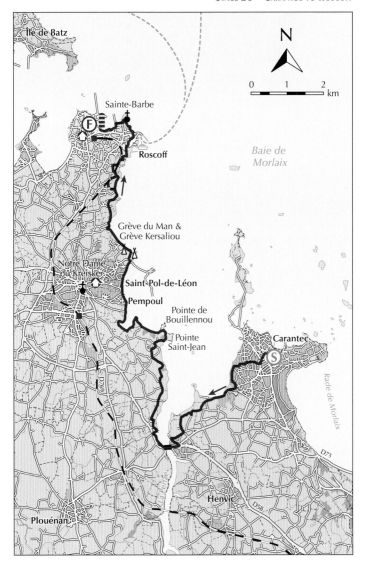

Île de Batz

Sainte-Barbe

F

Roscoff

Baie de Morlaix

N

0   1   2 km

Grève du Man & Grève Kersaliou

Notre Dame du Kreisker

Saint-Pol-de-Léon

Pempoul

Pointe de Bouillennou

Pointe Saint-Jean

Carantec

S

Rade de Morlaix

D769

La Pennzé

Henvic

D58

Plouénan

D71

and fork left. Turn right on a dirt road at a T-junction and, after 350 metres, make a hairpin right turn on a trail. After a brief passage through woods, the trail crosses open country. Turn left at a T-junction onto a surfaced road and right on Rue du Pen Ar Méen, followed by a right fork on Rue de Coatigariou, which leads to the water's edge. A left turn on Rue Jacques Gueguen brings a bridge over La Penzé River into view (**1hr**).

Cross the **bridge** and turn right on a surfaced path that descends into the woods close to the water. On reaching a road, turn right and right again onto a dirt road that returns to the water. Turn left here between buildings and right on a dirt road. Follow the road as it winds among houses, then turn right onto a larger road in open country.

Walk 1km beside this road and turn right on a dirt path beside a *lavoir*. Guided by a GR mark that points to the left, walk 50 metres across a field and then turn right down a tractor path. (There may be no mark for this right turn.) About halfway down the field, turn left on another path toward a group of houses in the distance. This path curves and reaches a surfaced road that leads to those houses.

Follow this road through the group of houses. After walking a short distance across fields, continue straight on a narrow path between other houses where the road curves left. After a right turn, the path emerges into the open and descends. Turn left at a T-junction and right onto a road (**2hr**).

Ahead lie two promontories – **Saint-Jean** and **Bouillennou** – that are not interesting for trekkers because vegetation obscures the view. Skip them by leaving the GR34 to walk on the road to a parking area. Walk through the parking area, turn left and continue 100 metres on a path across a field to rejoin the GR34.

Turn right to walk above Grève de Kervigou. The trail winds its way through fields. There are few GR marks here, but the route is obvious as it follows the coast. Cross a small dyke that separates a pond from the tidal beach and continue on a path next to a wall.

Walk beside a road along the coast to **Pempoul**, passing a picnic area and cafés/restaurants (**3hr**). To reach the centre of Saint-Pol-de-Léon from here (1.5km), follow Rue de la Rive.

> The Gulf Stream gives **Saint-Pol-de-Léon** a climate that favours market farming. This area produces 70% of the artichokes and 90% of the cauliflowers grown in France. The town was named for Paul Aurelien, a sixth-century Welsh monk who was one of the Founder Saints. He established monasteries and became the first bishop of the diocese of Léon. The graceful 15th-century belfry of Chapelle Notre Dame du Kreisker soars 79m into the sky – the tallest belfry in Brittany.

Pass two **campgrounds** to reach an embankment above a long beach: **Grève du Man and Grève Kersaliou**. ▸ Walk to the end of the embankment, then up steps to a path parallel to the beach behind a line of bushes. This path leads to a road: turn right, then left on a road that leads to Rue de Creac'h André.

At low tide, you can walk 1km along this beach to a ramp below Rue de Creac'h André.

Follow Rue de Creac'h André and Chemin de Kerfissiec through a residential area and back to the water. After walking 150 metres beside the water, you reach a parking area beside **Grande Grève**. The high-tide route from here, with GR marks, is shown as a variant on the map. If the tide is low, you can walk on the beach: after 350 metres, walk up concrete steps to leave the beach. Turn right at a T-junction onto Pors ar Bascon, and rejoin the GR34 (**4hr**).

Continue over a railway and turn right on **Rue de Ruveic**. This road passes under the railway after 100 metres, but the GR34 does not; instead, it turns left before the viaduct. Walk a further 150 metres and turn right to go under another viaduct. Turn left immediately on a dirt path before a parking area for the **Jardin Exotique**. Walk a short distance and turn right. Roscoff's pleasure craft harbour lies ahead. Turn left after 150 metres and walk down a winding path to a large parking area. Walk north through the parking area to the road that leads to the **Gare Maritime** (ferry terminal).

Cross the road and turn right to walk beside a parking area for vehicles awaiting the ferry. The GR34 leaves the port area on a trail that begins beside a water treatment plant. Initially, the trail passes through dense vegetation. Once in the open, you reach a simple, white **chapel** that is dedicated to Sainte Barbe, the patron saint of the Johnnie Onions.

ROSCOFF

Roscoff

In 1828, a Roscoff farmer named Henri Ollivier spotted a market opportunity: why not take a load of the pink onions that were grown in abundance here across the Channel to Britain and try selling them there? Ollivier's trip was a success, inspiring many others to follow him. Each year, after the Pardon de Sainte Barbe in July, Roscovites departed with loads of onions for Britain. These 'Johnnies', as the British called them, were well received. The amiable Johnnie Onion, peddling his onions door-to-door in Wales (speaking a language related to Welsh), England and even distant Scotland, found a place in popular imagination beside Roscoff's rapacious privateer and wily smuggler. They carried the onions in tresses on poles and later draped over heavily laden bicycles. In the 1920s, as many as 1400 Johnnies were selling 9000 tonnes of onions in Britain every year. The practice resumed after being interrupted by World War II, but declined in the face of the proliferation of supermarkets and other factors. (To learn more, visit the Maison des Johnnies in Roscoff.) Today, the 'Oignon de Roscoff' is an *Appellation d'Origine Protégée* (Protected Designation of Origin) within the EU, and if your local grocer does not have them, you can buy them online.

The sun sets slowly in the west; we bid a fond farewell to the GR34

After pausing to admire the view of Roscoff from the chapel, walk down to the embankment beside the harbour. The **Roscoff lighthouse**, standing on Quai d'Auxerre, is your final destination for this memorable trek on the GR34 along the North Brittany Coast.

Kenavo!

APPENDIX A

Four 5-day itineraries on the GR34

The following short treks fit within a week's holiday, including travel time from home to the starting point and back from the end point.

The Emerald Coast – Pointe du Grouin

Departing from Mont-Saint-Michel, this trek traces an arc around the bay, with a view of it all from Mont-Dol, and continues around the Pointe du Grouin to traverse the spectacular cliffs leading to Saint-Malo, an attractive city with a fabled history. An easy, pleasant coastal trail leads to Saint-Briac-sur-Mer. See Stages 1–5.

- Mont-Saint-Michel to Saint-Broladre (19.5km)
- Saint-Broladre to Cancale (30.5km)
- Cancale to La Guimorais (22km)
- La Guimorais to Saint-Malo (12.5km)
- Saint-Malo to Saint-Briac-sur-Mer (16km via 'sea bus' between Saint-Malo and Dinard)

Travel notes

- Train to Rennes (or ferry to Saint-Malo), then bus to Mont-Saint-Michel
- BreizhGo line 16 from Saint-Briac-sur-Mer to Saint-Malo, then train onwards (or ferry to UK)

The Emerald Coast – Cap Fréhel

Saint-Cast-le-Guildo is an animated town that attracts many holiday visitors. After passing Fort La Latte (which, perched on a rocky spur above the sea, looks impregnable but was not), you reach the magnificent Cap Fréhel. From there, you pass numerous beautiful beaches bordering the vast Baie de Saint-Brieuc. For variety, the GR34 goes inland up and down the Gouessant estuary. See Stages 7–11.

- Saint-Cast-le-Guildo to Petit Trécelin (17.5km)
- Petit Trécelin to Sables-d'Or-les-Pins (22km)
- Sables-d'Or-les-Pins to Pléneuf-Val-André (21km)
- Pléneuf-Val-André to Hillion (26.5km)
- Hillion to Saint-Brieuc (16km)

Travel notes

- Train (or ferry) to Saint-Malo, then BreizhGo line 14 to Saint-Cast-le-Guildo
- Train from Saint-Brieuc

The Pink Granite Coast

The extraordinary pink granite rocks along this section of the GR34 are arguably the most dazzling sight along the entire north Brittany coast, especially between Perros-Guirec and Ploumanac'h. See Stages 18–22.

- Tréguier to Port Blanc (29km)
- Port Blanc to Perros-Guirec (15km)
- Perros-Guirec to Trégastel (17.5km)
- Trégastel to Trébeurden (20km, following short-cut and omitting circuit of Île Grande)
- Trébeurden to Lannion (16km)

Travel notes

- Train to Lannion, then BreizhGo line 27 to Tréguier
- Train from Lannion

Morlaix Bay

This is the itinerary that was voted the favourite GR of the French. There is a variety of coastal walking – level trails close to the water and rigorous tracks that climb and descend steep slopes above the water – as well as forests and open fields. Don't miss Barnénez Cairn, the largest megalith in Europe, and enjoy a pause in Morlaix, an attractive city. See Stages 24–28.

- Locquirec to Plougasnou (20km)
- Plougasnou to Saint-Samson (13.5km)
- Saint-Samson to Morlaix (21km)
- Morlaix to Carantec (22.5km)
- Carantec to Saint-Pol-de-Léon (14.5km) or to Roscoff (20km)

Travel notes

- Train to Lannion, then TILT line 30 to Locquirec
- BreizhGo line 29 from Saint-Pol-de-Léon (or Roscoff) to Morlaix, then train onwards (or ferry from Roscoff to UK and Ireland)

APPENDIX B

Facilities table

Location	Distance from previous location (km)	Cumulative distance from start (km)	Accommodation	Refreshments	Shops
Mont-Saint-Michel	0.0	0.0	hotels	café/restaurants	yes
Quatre Salines	11.0	11.0	hotel, chambres d'hôtes	restaurant	
Roz-sur-Couesnon	1.0	12.0	hotel, chambres d'hôtes, campground	café/restaurant	
Saint-Marcan	4.5	16.5	chambres d'hôtes		
Saint-Broladre	3.0	19.5	chambres d'hôtes	café/restaurant	
Mont-Dol	13.0	32.5	hotel, chambres d'hôtes	café/restaurant	
Hirel	5.5	38.0	chambres d'hôtes	café/restaurant	yes
Saint-Benoît-des-Ondes	4.5	42.5	chambres d'hôtes	café/restaurants	yes
Cancale	7.5	50.0	hotels, chambres d'hôtes, youth hostel	café/restaurants	yes
Pointe de Grouin	7.5	57.5	hotel	restaurant	
La Guimorais	14.5	72.0	chambres d'hôtes	café/restaurants	
Rothéneuf	3.0	75.0		café/restaurants	yes
Saint-Malo	9.5	84.5	hotels, chambres d'hôtes, youth hostel	café/restaurants	yes

Location	Distance from previous location (km)	Cumulative distance from start (km)	Accommodation	Refreshments	Shops
Dinard (via Rance estuary)	13.5	98.0	hotels, chambres d'hôtes, campground	café/restaurants	yes
Saint-Lunaire	9.0	107.0	hotels, chambres d'hôtes	café/restaurants	yes
Saint-Briac-sur-Mer	8.0	115.0	hotels, chambres d'hôtes	café/restaurants	yes
Lancieux	3.0	118.0	hotel	café/restaurants	yes
Saint-Jacut-de-la-Mer	15.5	133.5	hotels	café/restaurants	yes
Le Guildo	4.0	137.5		café/restaurant	
Plage des Quatre Vaux	4.0	141.5		crêperie	
Saint-Cast-le-Guildo	9.0	150.5	hotels, chambres d'hôtes	café/restaurants	yes
Port-à-la-Duc	14.5	165.0		café/restaurant	
Petit Tréecelin	3.0	168.0	hotel	café/restaurant	
Fort La Latte	6.5	174.5			
Cap Fréhel	4.0	178.5		café	
Pléherel-Plage	6.5	185.0	hotel	café/restaurant	yes
Sables-d'Or-les-Pins	5.0	190.0	hotels, chambres d'hôtes, campground	café/restaurants	yes
Erquy	11.0	201.0	hotels, chambres d'hôtes	café/restaurants	yes
Pléneuf-Val-André	10.0	211.0	hotels, chambres d'hôtes	café/restaurants	yes

Location	Distance from previous location (km)	Cumulative distance from start (km)	Accommodation	Refreshments	Shops
Dahouët	3.0	214.0	chambres d'hôtes	café/restaurants	yes
Jospinet	7.0	221.0		restaurant	
Hillion	16.5	237.5	hotel	café/restaurants	yes
Yffiniac	4.5	242.0		crêperie	
Saint-Brieuc (3km)	9.0	251.0	hotels, chambres d'hôtes	café/restaurants	yes
Saint-Laurent-de-la-Mer	3.5	254.5	hotel	café/restaurant	yes
Les Rosaires	6.0	260.5		café/restaurants	
Binic	9.5	270.0	hotels, chambres d'hôtes	café/restaurants	yes
Portrieux	8.5	278.5	hotel	café/restaurants	yes
Saint-Quay-Portrieux	2.0	280.5	hotels, chambres d'hôtes	café/restaurants	yes
Saint-Marc	3.0	283.5		café	
Port Goret	2.0	285.5		café/restaurant	
Le Palus	2.0	287.5	hotel	café/restaurants	
Bréhec	13.0	300.5	chambres d'hôtes	café/restaurants	
Paimpol	21.0	321.5	hotels, chambres d'hôtes	café/restaurants	yes
Porz Even	6.0	327.5	hotel, chambres d'hôtes	café/restaurants	
l'Arcouest	4.0	331.5	hotels, chambres d'hôtes	café/restaurant	
Loguivy-de-la-Mer	5.0	336.5	hotel	café/restaurants	yes

Location	Distance from previous location (km)	Cumulative distance from start (km)	Accommodation	Refreshments	Shops
Lézardrieux	10.0	346.5	hotel, chambres d'hôtes	café/restaurants	yes
Kermouster	6.0	352.5		crêperie	
Laneros	8.5	361.0	campground		
Le Québo	4.5	365.5	chambres d'hôtes	café/restaurant	
Tréguier	20.0	385.5	hotels, chambres d'hôtes	café/restaurants	yes
La Roche Jaune	8.5	394.0		restaurant	
Porz Hir	7.5	401.5	campground	restaurant	
Anse de Gouermel	7.5	409.0	gîte d'étape	restaurant	
Buguélès	2.0	411.0	chambres d'hôtes		
Port Blanc	4.0	415.0	hotel, chambres d'hôtes, campground	café/restaurant	
Trestel	4.0	419.0	chambres d'hôtes	café/restaurants	
Port l'Epine	3.0	422.0	chambres d'hôtes	café/restaurant	
Perros-Guirec	8.0	430.0	hotels, chambres d'hôtes	café/restaurants	yes
Ploumanac'h	9.5	439.5	hotels, chambres d'hôtes	café/restaurants	yes
Trégastel (Coz Pors)	8.0	447.5	hotels, chambres d'hôtes	café/restaurants	yes
Landrellec	7.5	455.0	campground	café/restaurants	
Penvern	5.5	460.0	chambres d'hôtes	café/restaurant	

Location	Distance from previous location (km)	Cumulative distance from start (km)	Accommodation	Refreshments	Shops
Île Grande	9.5	470.0	chambres d'hôtes, campground	café/restaurant	shop
Trébeurden	7.0	477.0	hotels, chambres d'hôtes	café/restaurants	yes
Beg Léguer	7.0	484.0	chambres d'hôtes	café/restaurant	
Lannion	9.0	493.0	hotels, chambres d'hôtes	café/restaurants	yes
Le Yaudet	7.5	500.5	chambres d'hôtes	café/restaurant	
Locquémeau	5.0	505.5	chambres d'hôtes, campground	café/restaurant	
Saint-Michel-en-Grève	6.5	512.0	chambres d'hôtes	café/restaurant	
Saint-Efflam	4.0	516.0		café	
Beg Douar	2.5	518.5	hotel	café	
Toul an Héry	4.5	523.0	chambres d'hôtes	crêperie	
Locquirec	4.5	527.5	hotels, chambres d'hôtes, campground	café/restaurant	yes
Moulin de la Rive	4.0	531.5		café/restaurant	
Poul Rodou	2.5	534.0		café/restaurant	
Saint-Jean-du-Doigt (1km from Plage de Saint-Jean-du-Doigt)	12.0	546.0	campground	crêperie	shop

Location	Distance from previous location (km)	Cumulative distance from start (km)	Accommodation	Refreshments	Shops
Plougasnou (400 metres from Ker Maria)	1.0	547.0	hotel, chambres d'hôtes	café/restaurant	yes
Primel-Trégastel	3.5	550.5	chambres d'hôtes	café/restaurants	
Le Diben	5.0	555.5	hotels, chambres d'hôtes	café/restaurants	yes
Saint-Samson	5.0	560.5	gîte d'étape	café/restaurant	
Térénez	2.0	562.5	chambres d'hôtes	café/restaurants	
Dourduff-en-Mer	11.5	574.0		café/restaurant	
Morlaix	7.5	581.5	hotels, chambres d'hôtes, youth hostel	café/restaurants	yes
Locquénolé	13.5	595.0	chambres d'hôtes	café/restaurants	yes
Carantec	9.0	604.0	hotels, chambres d'hôtes	café/restaurants	yes
Pempoul	12.0	616.0		café/restaurants	
Saint-Pol-de-Léon (1.5km from Pempoul)	612.5		hotels, chambres d'hôtes	café/restaurants	yes
Roscoff	8.0	624.0	hotels, chambres d'hôtes	café/restaurants	yes

Note: campgrounds listed here are those that may offer accommodation to trekkers without camping gear.

APPENDIX C
Accommodation

Options for accommodation along the GR34 are abundant, albeit unevenly distributed, reflecting the play of supply and demand in the tourist industry. There are many online sources of information that will be invaluable for the GR34 trekker, starting with tourist offices (see Appendix E). This appendix provides a selection of accommodation, focusing on areas where the options are more limited and including places that offer a warm welcome to trekkers. There are many campgrounds close to the GR34; those included here may offer accommodation to trekkers without camping gear. When calling a phone number from outside France, add the country code (33) and omit the initial 0.

General information
www.tourismebretagne.com (English-language option: 'Plan my holiday', 'Where to stay?')

https://rando-etapes.bzh ('Hébergements', 'GR34 le sentier des douaniers')

www.rando-accueil.com ('Hébergements', 'Dans quelle region?', 'Bretagne')

Campgrounds
www.brittanytourism.com (English-language option: 'Plan my holiday', 'Where to stay?', 'Campsites')

Stage 1
Mont-Saint-Michel
See www.ot-montsaintmichel.com (English-language option: 'Plan your stay', 'Our accommodations')

Fleur de Sel
Roz-sur-Couesnon
tel 02 99 80 20 60
www.demeure-fleurdesel.com

Les Quatre Salines
Roz-sur-Couesnon

tel 02 99 80 23 80
www.hotel-les-4-salines.com

Camping Les Couesnons
Roz-sur-Couesnon
tel 02 99 80 26 86
https://lescouesnons.com

Les Fleurettes
Saint-Marcan
tel 02 99 80 28 93
www.lesfleurettes.fr

Le Petit Angle (1km from Saint-Broladre)
tel 02 99 80 00 26
tel 06 71 26 80 93
www.lepetitangle.fr

Stage 2
Hôtel du Tertre
Mont-Dol
tel 02 99 48 20 57
www.hoteldutertre.com

Le Petit Châtelet
Hirel
tel 02 99 48 96 29
tel 06 60 25 34 94
www.petitchatelet.com

Le Domaine
Hirel
tel 02 99 48 95 61
tel 06 31 52 91 79
https://le-domaine.fr

La Grande Mare
Saint-Benoît-des-Ondes
tel 02 99 19 77 92
www.lagrandemare.fr

La Ville Es Gris
Cancale
tel 02 99 89 67 27
tel 06 60 43 45 05
www.gitesetchambresdemer.fr

Le Querrien
Cancale
tel 02 99 89 64 56
www.le-querrien.com

Le Cancalais
Cancale
tel 02 99 89 61 93
www.lecancalais.fr

Auberge de Jeunesse
Cancale
tel 02 99 89 62 62
www.hifrance.org
(select 'Cancale – Baie Mont St-Michel'
from the drop-down list)

Stage 3
Chapijemi
La Guimorais
tel 02 99 89 07 03
tel 06 87 47 45 50
http://chapijemi.eu

Stage 4
Saint-Malo
See www.saint-malo-tourisme.co.uk

Auberge de jeunesse Patrick Varangot
Saint-Malo
tel 02 99 40 29 80
https://tourisme.ty-al-levenez.fr

Stage 5
Dinard
See www.dinardemeraudetourisme.com
('Séjourner', 'Où dormir?')

Brit Hotel
Dinard
tel 02 99 46 11 39
https://hotel-dinard-tourelles.brithotel.fr

Camping du Port Blanc
Dinard
tel 02 99 46 10 74
www.camping-Port-Blanc.com

Hôtel Kan-avel
Saint-Lunaire
tel 02 99 46 30 13
www.kan-avel.fr

Le Brise-Lames
Saint-Briac-sur-Mer
tel 02 99 88 39 99
http://lebriselames.free.fr

Hôtel des Bains
Lancieux
tel 02 96 86 31 33
http://hotel-des-bains-lancieux.fr

Stage 6
Abbaye Saint-Jacut
Saint-Jacut-de-la-Mer
tel 02 96 27 71 19
www.abbaye-st-jacut.com

Le Vieux Moulin
Saint-Jacut-de-la-Mer
tel 02 96 27 71 02
tel 06 72 81 58 99
www.hotel-le-vieux-moulin.com

La Cerisaie
Saint-Cast-le-Guildo
tel 06 03 96 00 38
https://lacerisaie.cleasite.fr

Le Port-Jacquet
Saint-Cast-le-Guildo
tel 02 96 41 97 18
www.port-jacquet.com

Stage 7
Le Trécelin
Le Petit Trécelin
tel 02 96 41 46 82
www.hoteltrecelin.com

Stage 8
Kerléon
Plévenon
tel 09 86 31 74 68
tel 06 15 28 37 35
https://kerleon.fr

Auberge l'Air de Vent
Pléhérel-Plage
tel 02 96 41 41 01
www.aubergelairdevent.com

Les Mimosas
Sables-d'Or-les-Pins
tel 02 96 41 56 81

Hôtel de Diane
Sables-d'Or-les-Pins
tel 02 96 41 42 07
www.hoteldiane.fr

Camping Les Salines (Plurien)
Sables-d'Or-les-Pins
tel 02 96 72 17 40
tel 06 28 22 43 36
www.campinglessalines.fr

Stage 9
Les Bruyères d'Erquy
Erquy
tel 06 81 85 55 46
https://lesbruyeres-erquy.com

Hôtel de la Mer
Pléneuf-Val-André
tel 02 96 72 20 44
http://hotel-de-la-mer.pleneuf-val-andre.
hotels-fr.net/en

Stage 10
Chambres d'Hôtes L'Agapanthe
Dahouët
tel 084 33 89 51
https://lagapanthe.business.site

Le Nid de la Baie
Morieux (1km off route)
tel 09 53 47 10 48
tel 06 99 80 10 60
www.leniddelabaie.com

Le Logis des Grenouilles
Morieux (1km off route)
tel 06 87 59 25 11
https://mariepauleperigois22.jimdofree.
com

Au Bon Saint-Nicolas
Hillion
tel 02 96 32 21 03
www.au-bon-saint-nicolas.com

Stage 11
Saint-Brieuc
See www.baiedesaintbrieuc.com/en/
bay-accommodation

Le Clos Laurentais
Saint-Laurent-de-la-Mer (Plérin)
tel 02 96 73 03 38
tel 06 29 25 81 39
www.hotel-lecloslaurentais-plerin.com

Stage 12
Le Neptune
Binic
tel 02 96 73 61 02
www.hotel-restaurant-leneptune-binic.fr

Chambre d'Hôtes Bretagne Binic
Binic
tel 06 20 02 44 75
www.bretagnebinic.com

Le Benhuyc
Binic
tel 02 96 78 79 79
www.lebenhuyc.com

Tagar Étape
Étables-sur-Mer (1km off route)
tel 07 68 40 55 08
www.tagaretape.fr

Le Kreisker
Saint-Quay-Portrieux
tel 02 96 70 57 84
www.hotelkreisker.com

Stage 13
Chez Paulette
Le Paulus
tel 02 96 70 38 26
http://chezpauletteplouha.free.fr

Le Saint Roc'h
Lanloup (1km off route)
tel 02 96 22 33 55
www.rando-accueil.com (search 'Saint Roch')

Camping Le Neptune
Lanloup (1km off route)
tel 02 96 22 33 35
www.leneptune.com

Le Beau Rivage
Bréhec
tel 02 96 55 07 61
www.beau-rivage-brehec.com

Stage 14
Camping Cap de Bréhat
Port Lazo
tel 02 57 79 00 12
www.cap-de-brehat.com

Paimpol
See www.guingamp-paimpol.com/en ('My stay', 'Accommodation')

Stage 15
Les Agapanthes
Ploubazlanec (1km off route)
tel 02 96 55 89 06
www.hotel-les-agapanthes.com

Hôtel Bocher
Porz Even
tel 02 96 55 84 16
www.hotelbocher.com

Le Relais de Launay
Porz Even
tel 02 96 55 86 30
www.relaisdelaunay.com

Les Terrasses de Bréhat
Pointe de l'Arcouest
tel 02 96 55 77 92
https://terrasses-brehat.fr

Au Grand Large
Loguivy-de-la-Mer
tel 02 96 20 90 18
tel 02 96 20 87 10
www.hotelrestaurant-augrandlarge.com

Côte de Granit Rose
See www.brittany-pinkgranitcoast.co.uk (select 'My stay' from the menu)

Le Littoral
Lézardrieux
tel 02 96 20 10 59
www.hotel-lelittoral.com

Stage 16
Rando Gîte de Lanmodez
Lanmodez (1.5km off route)
tel 06 80 76 8176
https://gitelanmodez.fr

Baradoz ar mor
L'Armor
tel 02 96 20 68 03
tel 06 51 74 37 33
tel 07 69 73 60 90
www.baradozarmor.fr

Camping Domaine de Laneros
Laneros
tel 02 96 55 58 63
tel 07 87 14 81 82
www.camping-laneros.com
('Randonneurs GR34')

Stage 17
L'Abri du Sillon (gîte d'étape)
Pleubian (2km off route)
tel 06 17 46 17 98
www.abri-du-sillon.com

Les Chambres du Sillon
Pleubian (2km off route)
tel 06 76 58 16 19
http://les-chambres-d-hotes-du-sillon-
bed-breakfast.allbrittanyhotels.com/en

Le Saint-Yves
Tréguier
tel 02 96 92 33 49
tel 06 62 30 80 75
www.lesaintyvestreguier.com

L'Estuaire
Tréguier
tel 02 96 92 30 25
www.hotelestuairetreguier.fr

Chambres d'Hôtes du Cloître
Tréguier
tel 07 69 25 75 87

www.brittany-pinkgranitcoast.co.uk
(search 'B&B le Cloître')

Chambres d'Hôtes, Mme Augès
Tréguier
tel 06 60 33 52 52
tel 06 60 82 36 67
www.brittany-pinkgranitcoast.co.uk
(search 'Catherine Augès')

Stage 18
L'Escale
(1km from Plougrescant)
tel 02 96 92 58 38
tel 06 44 08 89 78
www.brittanytourism.com (search
'L'Escale')

Camping Le Varlen (500m)
Porz Hir
tel 02 96 92 52 15
www.levarlen.com (search
'Randonneurs')

Gîte d'étape Da Gousket (500m from
GR34)
Gouermel
tel 02 96 11 84 95
tel 06 86 61 29 97
www.pour-les-vacances.com/site-11816

Chambres d'Hôtes, M Henry
Buguélès
tel 02 96 92 82 76
www.invitation-au-rivage.fr

Le Grand Hôtel
Port Blanc
tel 096 92 66 52
www.grandhotelportblanc.com

Chambres d'Hôtes, Mme Le Tynevez
Port Blanc
tel 06 15 33 94 10

Camping Les Hauts de Port Blanc (2km)
Port Blanc
tel 07 83 47 53 83
www.portblanc.com/
campsite-france-brittany-trekkers

Stage 19
Les Hortensias
Trestel
tel 06 87 35 19 10
tel 02 90 27 00 22
www.leshortensias22.fr

Les Sternes
Louannec
tel 02 96 91 03 38
www.sternes.com

Perros-Guirec
See http://tourisme.perros-guirec.com/
sejournez.html

Au Bon Accueil
Perros-Guirec
tel 02 96 23 25 77
www.aubonaccueil-hotel.fr

Stage 20
Le Phare
Ploumanac'h
tel 02 96 91 41 19
www.hotel-le-phare.fr

L'Europe
Ploumanac'h
tel 02 96 91 40 76
https://hoteldeleurope-perros.com

Chambre d'Hôtes Ti Mina
Ploumanac'h
tel 02 96 91 66 31
tel 06 81 15 80 96
www.chambres-hotes.fr (search 'Ti
Mina' in 'Destination')

Bellevue
Trégastel
tel 02 96 23 88 18
https://hotelbellevuetregastel.com

Hôtel de la Mer
Trégastel
tel 02 96 15 60 00
www.hoteldelamer-tregastel.com

Stage 21
Camping Municipal
Landrellec
tel 02 96 23 87 92
www.pleumeur-bodou.com/
camping-municipal-de-landrellec

Camping Municipal du Dourlin
Île Grande
tel 02 96 91 92 41
www.pleumeur-bodou.com/
Camping-Municipal-du-Dourlin

La Bergerie
Île Grande
tel 06 11 36 49 36
www.labergerie-ig.fr

Rêves de Mer – Centre du Baly
Île Grande
tel 02 96 91 95 06
www.revesdemer.com/
nos-etablissements/
centre-dhebergement-le-baly

Stage 22
Auberge Granit Rose
Trébeurden
tel 02 96 23 52 22
www.aubergegranitrose.fr

Le Toëno
Trébeurden
tel 02 96 23 68 78
www.hoteltoeno.com

L'Écume de Mer
Trébeurden
tel 02 96 23 50 60
www.lecumedemer.fr

Chambres d'Hôtes Mme Le Guillouzic
Trébeurden
tel 02 96 23 59 01
tel 06 63 51 80 89
http://chambredhotes-trebeurden.com

La Maison
Trébeurden
tel 02 96 15 43 18
www.lamaisontrebeurden.fr

Chambres d'Hôtes Kersilio
Beg Léguer
tel 06 20 16 79 80
www.chambres-hotes.fr/chambres-
hotes_vue-mer-plage-et-gr34-
accessible-a-pied_lannion_54994.htm

Chambres d'Hôtes Ar Prioldi
Lannion
tel 02 96 48 04 25
tel 06 81 86 98 41
www.brittany-pinkgranitcoast.co.uk
(search 'Ar Prioldi')

Chambres d'Hôtes Au Joli Bois
Lannion
tel 02 96 37 91 70
tel 06 84 42 06 61
www.brittany-pinkgranitcoast.co.uk
(search 'Le Joli Bois')

Entre Terre et Mer
Lannion
tel 02 96 45 74 95
tel 06 74 97 95 24
www.brittany-pinkgranitcoast.co.uk
(search 'Entre Terre et Mer')

Cerise
Lannion
tel 02 96 37 51 18

tel 06 36 97 28 73
www.brittany-pinkgranitcoast.co.uk
(search 'Cerise')

Hôtel ibis Lannion Côte de Granit Rose
Lannion
tel 02 96 37 03 67
https://www.brittany-pinkgranitcoast.
co.uk (search 'Ibis')

Le Yaudet
tel 02 96 46 48 80
www.le-yaudet.fr

Stage 23
Chambres d'Hôtes Le Run Ar Mor
Locquémeau
tel 02 96 35 21 40
www.brittany-pinkgranitcoast.co.uk
(search 'Run Ar Mor')

La Vie en Rose
Saint-Michel-en-Grèves
tel 06 49 93 93 68
tel 02 96 23 08 36
www.brittany-pinkgranitcoast.co.uk
(search 'La Vie en Rose')

Chambres d'Hôtes
Kermorvan
tel 02 96 23 13 51
tel 06 02 05 80 20
www.maggie-kermorvan.com

Hôtel Les Panoramas
Beg Douar
tel 02 96 35 63 76
www.lespanoramas.fr

Chambres d'Hôtes – Plestin les Grèves
Toul An Héry
tel 02 96 54 19 59
tel 06 20 41 37 75
www.chambres-hotes.fr (search 'Plestin-
les-Grèves' in 'Destination')

Chambres d'Hôtes Keric an Oll
Locquirec
tel 02 98 79 34 61
www.chambres-hotes.fr (search 'Keric
an Oll' in 'Destination')

Camping du Fond de la Baie
Locquirec
tel 02 98 67 40 85
www.campinglocquirec.com

Hôtel du Port
Locquirec
tel 02 98 15 32 98
www.hotelduport-locquirec.fr

Stage 24
Baie de Morlaix
See www.baiedemorlaix.bzh/en/
hebergement

Escale de Trobodec
Prajou (700m off route)
tel 06 84 68 10 18
https://escaledetrobodec.wordpress.com

Camping de Pont Ar Gler
Saint-Jean-du-Doigt (1km off route)
tel 02 98 67 32 15
https://campingstj.jimdofree.com

Le Relai de la Plume
Plougasnou
tel 02 98 67 32 22
www.relaisdelaplume.com

Stage 25
La Cameline
Primel-Trégastel
tel 02 98 72 38 81
www.la-cameline.com

Le Carnet de Bord
Le Diben
tel 06 24 69 33 54
https://legiteducarnetdebord.wordpress.
com

Le Fournil De Penn Ar Bed
Le Diben
tel 02 98 72 44 24
tel 06 71 16 33 72
www.fournildepennarbed.com

Au Temps des Voiles
Le Diben
tel 02 98 72 32 43
www.autempsdesvoiles.com

La Maison de Kerdiès
Saint-Samson
tel 02 98 72 40 66
www.maisonkerdies.com

Stage 26
Chambres d'Hôtes Á BORD!
Térénez
tel 06 56 74 19 04
https://abord.vpweb.fr

Camping de la Baie de Térénez
Plouézoc'h
tel 02 98 67 26 80
www.campingbaiedeterenez.com

Le Logis du Port
Morlaix
tel 06 07 68 36 68
www.lelogisduport.fr

Les Chambres de Guernisac
Morlaix
tel 06 99 44 52 06
www.chambres-guernisac.bzh

Le Saint Melaine
Morlaix
tel 02 98 88 54 76
www.hotel-saint-melaine.com

Hôtel du Port
Morlaix
tel 02 98 88 07 54
www.hotelduport-morlaix.com

Auberge de Jeunesse
Morlaix
tel 02 98 15 10 55
www.aj-morlaix.org

Stage 27
Demeure des Tilleuls
Locquénolé
tel 02 22 55 19 96
tel 06 14 16 64 47
www.chambredhoteslocquenole.com

Ti'Case
Carantec
tel 06 62 13 60 67
https://chambreticase.com

Hôtel de la Baie de Morlaix
Carantec
tel 02 98 67 07 64
www.hotel-baiedemorlaix.com

Les Chambres du Mad
Carantec
Lieu-dit Keryénévet (Henvic)
tel 02 98 19 20 76
https://chambresdumad.jimdofree.com

Stage 28
Saint-Pol-de-Léon (1.5km off route)
See www.saintpoldeleon.fr/
hebergement-touristique

Roscoff
See www.roscoff-tourisme.com/en/
accomodation

Hôtel d'Angleterre
Roscoff
tel 02 98 69 70 42
www.hotel-angleterre-roscoff.fr

Les Arcades
Roscoff
tel 02 98 69 70 45
www.hotel-les-arcades-roscoff.com

Les Chardons Bleus
Roscoff
tel 02 98 69 72 03
www.hotel-chardons-bleus.com

Chez Janie
Roscoff
tel 02 98 61 24 25
www.chezjanie.fr

APPENDIX D
Transport

Ferry services
Brittany Ferries
www.brittany-ferries.co.uk

Condor Ferries
www.condorferries.co.uk

Saint-Malo–Dinard
https://compagniecorsaire.com

Rail (SNCF)
National
https://en.oui.sncf/en

Regional
www.ter.sncf.com/bretagne

Buses
Listed below are the most helpful bus services for walkers on the Brittany Coast Path (as mentioned in the information boxes at the beginning of each stage), along with some of the towns served by the lines.

Keolis Armor
https://keolis-armor.com/en/5ey-Going-to-Mont-Saint-Michel.html
• Rennes to Mont-Saint-Michel
• Saint-Malo to Mont-Saint-Michel

Pontorson–Mont-Saint-Michel shuttle bus
www.bienvenueaumontsaint michel.com/en/preparing-your-visit/arriving-by-train

BreizhGo (inter-city)
www.breizhgo.bzh/se-deplacer-en-bretagne ('En car')
En Ille-et-Vilaine:
• **16:** Saint-Briac – Dinard – Saint-Malo
• **17:** (summer): Roz-sur-Couesnon – Saint-Broladre – Hirel – Cancale – Saint-Malo
En Côtes d'Armor:
• **1:** Saint-Brieuc – Binic – Saint-Quay-Portrieux – Bréhec – Paimpol
• **2:** Erquy – Pléneuf – Hillion – Saint-Brieuc (summer: Saint-Cast-le-Guildo – Pléhérel-Plage – Sables-d'Or)
• **14:** Saint-Malo – Lancieux – Saint-Jacut-de-la-Mer – Saint-Cast-le-Guildo
• **25:** Paimpol – Lézardrieux – Lanmodez – Pleubian
• **27:** Paimpol – Lézardrieux – Tréguier – Lannion
En Finistère:
• **29:** Roscoff – Saint-Pol-de-Léon – Morlaix

MAT (Saint-Malo)
www.reseau-mat.fr (select 'Getting around', 'Routes and timetables')
• **9:** (summer: Cancale – Pointe du Grouin – La Guimorais) Rothéneuf – Saint-Malo

TUB (Saint-Brieuc)

https://tub.bzh
- **20:** Hillion – Saint-Brieuc
- **D:** Saint-Brieuc – Port du Légué – Saint-Laurent-de-la-Mer

TILT (Lannion)

www.lannion-tregor.com (select 'Déplacements', 'Le réseau urbain et péri-urbain')
- **D:** Trégastel – Penvern – Île Grande – Trébeurden – Lannion
- **E:** Lannion – Perros-Guirec – Ploumanac'h – Trégastel
- **M:** (Thursdays): Penvénan – Port Blanc – Lannion

- **Macareux:** Perros-Guirec – Ploumanac'h – Trégastel
- **30:** Lannion – Saint-Michel-en-Grève – Saint-Efflam – Locquirec – Morlaix

Linéotim (Morlaix)

www.lineotim.com
- **20:** Saint-Jean-du-Doigt – Plougasnou – Le Diben – Saint-Samson – Cairn de Barnénez – Dourduff-en-Mer – Morlaix
- **28:** Morlaix – Locquénolé – Carantec

APPENDIX E
Useful contacts

Tourist information

Brittany
www.tourismebretagne.com

GR34 – Sentier des douaniers ('the customs officers' path')
www.tourismebretagne.com
(search 'GR34')

Mont-Saint-Michel
www.ot-montsaintmichel.com

Saint-Broladre
http://tourisme.saint-broladre.fr

Mont Dol
www.mont-dol.fr

Cancale
www.ville-cancale.fr

Saint-Malo
www.saint-malo-tourisme.co.uk

Dinard
www.dinardemeraudetourisme.com

Dinan–Cap Fréhel
www.dinan-capfrehel.com/en

Cap d'Erquy–Val André
www.capderquy-valandre.com/en

Saint-Brieuc Bay
www.baiedesaintbrieuc.com/en

Binic
www.binic-etables-sur-mer.fr/office-de-tourisme

Saint-Quay-Portrieux
www.saintquayportrieux.com/en

Paimpol
www.guingamp-paimpol.com/en

Lézardrieux
www.mairie-lezardrieux.fr/tourisme.html

Tréguier
www.ville-treguier.fr

Perros-Guirec
www.perros-guirec.com

Côte de Granit Rose
www.brittany-pinkgranitcoast.co.uk

Le Yaudet
www.ploulech.fr (search 'site du Yaudet')

Morlaix Bay
www.baiedemorlaix.bzh/en

Saint-Pol-de-Léon
www.saintpoldeleon.fr

Roscoff
www.roscoff-tourisme.com/en

Maps and information about routes

Institut Géographique National
(French mapping authority)
www.ign.fr

Stanfords
(Map retailer based in London and Bristol)
www.stanfords.co.uk

The Map Shop
(Map retailer based in Upton-upon-Severn)
www.themapshop.co.uk

Omni Resources
(Map retailer based in Burlington, NC, USA)
www.omnimap.com

Fédération Française de la Randonnée Pédestre (FFRP)
(French national hiking association)
www.ffrandonnee.fr

Mon GR
(Guide for GR trails in France, published by FFRP)
www.mongr.fr (search 'GR34' and select the 'Itinéraire' option)

Itirando
(Guide for hiking in Brittany)
https://itirando.bzh

Au Vieux Campeur
(Retailer for clothing and equipment in Paris and other French cities)
www.auvieuxcampeur.fr

Weather forecasts
meteoblue
www.meteoblue.com

Météo France
https://meteofrance.com/applications-mobiles

The Weather Channel
https://weather.com/fr

Emergencies
European emergency number 112

APPENDIX F
Glossary

Useful phrases

English	French
Hello	Bonjour
Please	S'il vous plaît (SVP)
Thank you	Merci
Good morning	Bonjour
Good evening	Bonsoir, bonne soirée
Good night	Bonne nuit
Goodbye	Au revoir
Do you speak English?	Parlez-vous anglais?
I don't understand	Je ne comprends pas
Where is…?	Où est…? Où se trouve…?
the railway/train station	la gare
the bus station	la gare routière
the ferry terminal	la gare maritime
a bakery	une boulangerie
a pastry shop	une pâtisserie
a food shop, grocer's	une épicerie

English	French
a chemist, drug store	une pharmacie
a hotel	un hôtel
a B&B	une chambres d'hôtes
I would like a room (with bath/ shower)	Je voudrais une chambre (avec bain/ douche)
How much…?	Combien?
café	café
restaurant	restaurant, brasserie
bill, check	addition
service included	service compris
Enjoy your meal!	Bon appétit!

On the trail

French	English
ajonc	gorse
algue verte	algae
anse	cove
averse	(rain) shower
baie	bay
balise	buoy

French	English
bateau de pêche, plaisance	fishing boat, pleasure boat
brise-lames	breakwater, jetty
brouillard	fog
bruine	drizzle
brume	mist
bruyère	heather
caillou	pebble
chaos de rochers	blockfield, boulder field
corps de garde	watch house
côte, côtier	coast, coastal
digue	dyke
douanier	customs officer
dune	dune
eau douce	fresh water
eau de mer	seawater, saltwater
éboulement	rockfall, mudslide
échouer, échouage	to ground, grounding
école de voile	sailing school
écluse	lock
embruns	spray
escarpé	steep
estran	foreshore (between high & low tide)
estuaire	estuary
falaise	cliff
fougère	fern, bracken
galet	pebble, stone
genêt	broom (bot.)

French	English
glisser, glissant	to slip, slippery
goémon	seaweed
granit (rose)	(pink) granite
grès	sandstone
grève	shore
houle	swell (waves)
île, îlot	island, islet
lande	moor, heath
large (n.)	open sea
lavoir	wash-house
littoral	coast, coastal
maître-nageur	lifeguard
Manche	(English) Channel
marée (haute, basse, grande)	tide (high, low, spring)
marnage	tidal range
mer	sea
mouillage	anchorage
nuage	cloud
pêche	fishing
péninsule, presqu'île	peninsula
phare	lighthouse
pierre	stone
plage	beach
planche à voile	windsurfing (board)
pluie	rain
pont	bridge
port	harbour, port
poste de secours	first aid post
pointe	headland
quai	quay

French	English
rade	harbour, roads
ria	ria
rivière	river
rocher	rock, boulder
ronce	bramble
sable	sand
soleil	sun
sémaphore	coastal surveillance station
sentier	trail, path

French	English
table d'orientation	map table
tempête	storm
temps	weather
tertre	mound
tourbe	peat
variante	variant
vague	wave
voilier	sailboat

LISTING OF CICERONE GUIDES

BRITISH ISLES CHALLENGES, COLLECTIONS AND ACTIVITIES
Cycling Land's End to John o' Groats
The Big Rounds
The Book of the Bivvy
The Book of the Bothy
The Mountains of England & Wales:
 Vol 1 Wales
 Vol 2 England
The National Trails
Walking The End to End Trail

SCOTLAND
Ben Nevis and Glen Coe
Cycle Touring in Northern Scotland
Cycling in the Hebrides
Great Mountain Days in Scotland
Mountain Biking in Southern and Central Scotland
Mountain Biking in West and North West Scotland
Not the West Highland Way Scotland
Scotland's Best Small Mountains
Scotland's Mountain Ridges
Skye's Cuillin Ridge Traverse
The Borders Abbeys Way
The Great Glen Way
The Great Glen Way Map Booklet
The Hebridean Way
The Hebrides
The Isle of Mull
The Isle of Skye
The Skye Trail
The Southern Upland Way
The Speyside Way
The Speyside Way Map Booklet
The West Highland Way
The West Highland Way Map Booklet
Walking Ben Lawers, Rannoch and Atholl
Walking in the Cairngorms
Walking in the Pentland Hills
Walking in the Scottish Borders
Walking in the Southern Uplands
Walking in Torridon
Walking Loch Lomond and the Trossachs
Walking on Arran
Walking on Harris and Lewis
Walking on Jura, Islay and Colonsay
Walking on Rum and the Small Isles
Walking on the Orkney and Shetland Isles
Walking on Uist and Barra

Walking the Cape Wrath Trail
Walking the Corbetts
 Vol 1 South of the Great Glen
 Vol 2 North of the Great Glen
Walking the Galloway Hills
Walking the Munros
 Vol 1 – Southern, Central and Western Highlands
 Vol 2 – Northern Highlands and the Cairngorms
Winter Climbs Ben Nevis and Glen Coe
Winter Climbs in the Cairngorms

NORTHERN ENGLAND ROUTES
Cycling the Reivers Route
Cycling the Way of the Roses
Hadrian's Cycleway
Hadrian's Wall Path
Hadrian's Wall Path Map Booklet
The C2C Cycle Route
The Pennine Way
The Pennine Way Map Booklet
The Coast to Coast Walk
The Coast to Coast Map Booklet
Walking the Dales Way
Walking the Dales Way Map Booklet

NORTH EAST ENGLAND, YORKSHIRE DALES AND PENNINES
Cycling in the Yorkshire Dales
Great Mountain Days in the Pennines
Mountain Biking in the Yorkshire Dales
St Oswald's Way and St Cuthbert's Way
The Cleveland Way and the Yorkshire Wolds Way
The Cleveland Way Map Booklet
The North York Moors
The Reivers Way
The Teesdale Way
Trail and Fell Running in the Yorkshire Dales
Walking in County Durham
Walking in Northumberland
Walking in the North Pennines
Walking in the Yorkshire Dales: North and East
Walking in the Yorkshire Dales: South and West

NORTH WEST ENGLAND AND THE ISLE OF MAN
Cycling the Pennine Bridleway
Isle of Man Coastal Path
The Lancashire Cycleway
The Lune Valley and Howgills

Walking in Cumbria's Eden Valley
Walking in Lancashire
Walking in the Forest of Bowland and Pendle
Walking on the Isle of Man
Walking on the West Pennine Moors
Walks in Silverdale and Arnside

LAKE DISTRICT
Cycling in the Lake District
Great Mountain Days in the Lake District
Joss Naylor's Lakes, Meres and Waters of the Lake District
Lake District Winter Climbs
Lake District: High Level and Fell Walks
Lake District: Low Level and Lake Walks
Mountain Biking in the Lake District
Outdoor Adventures with Children – Lake District
Scrambles in the Lake District – North
Scrambles in the Lake District – South
The Cumbria Way
Trail and Fell Running in the Lake District
Walking the Lake District Fells –
 Borrowdale
 Buttermere
 Coniston
 Keswick
 Langdale
 Mardale and the Far East
 Patterdale
 Wasdale
Walking the Tour of the Lake District

DERBYSHIRE, PEAK DISTRICT AND MIDLANDS
Cycling in the Peak District
Dark Peak Walks
Scrambles in the Dark Peak
Walking in Derbyshire
Walking in the Peak District – White Peak East
Walking in the Peak District – White Peak West

SOUTHERN ENGLAND
20 Classic Sportive Rides in South East England
20 Classic Sportive Rides in South West England
Cycling in the Cotswolds
Mountain Biking on the North Downs

Mountain Biking on the
  South Downs
Walking the South West Coast
  Path
South West Coast Path Map
  Booklets Vol 1: Minehead to
  St Ives
    Vol 2: St Ives to Plymouth
    Vol 3: Plymouth to Poole
Suffolk Coast and Heath Walks
The Cotswold Way
The Cotswold Way Map Booklet
The Great Stones Way
The Kennet and Avon Canal
The Lea Valley Walk
The North Downs Way
The North Downs Way Map
  Booklet
The Peddars Way and Norfolk
  Coast path
The Pilgrims' Way
The Ridgeway National Trail
The Ridgeway Map Booklet
The South Downs Way
The South Downs Way Map
  Booklet
The Thames Path
The Thames Path Map Booklet
The Two Moors Way
The Two Moors Way Map Booklet
Walking Hampshire's Test Way
Walking in Cornwall
Walking in Essex
Walking in Kent
Walking in London
Walking in Norfolk
Walking in the Chilterns
Walking in the Cotswolds
Walking in the Isles of Scilly
Walking in the New Forest
Walking in the North Wessex
  Downs
Walking on Dartmoor
Walking on Guernsey
Walking on Jersey
Walking on the Isle of Wight
Walking the Jurassic Coast
Walks in the South Downs
  National Park

WALES AND WELSH BORDERS

Cycle Touring in Wales
Cycling Lon Las Cymru
Glyndwr's Way
Great Mountain Days in
  Snowdonia
Hillwalking in Shropshire
Hillwalking in Wales – Vols 1&2
Mountain Walking in Snowdonia
Offa's Dyke Path
Offa's Dyke Map Booklet
Ridges of Snowdonia
Scrambles in Snowdonia

Snowdonia: 30 Low-level and easy
  walks – North
Snowdonia: 30 Low-level and easy
  walks – South
The Cambrian Way
The Ceredigion and Snowdonia
  Coast Paths
The Pembrokeshire Coast Path
The Pembrokeshire Coast Path
  Map Booklet
The Severn Way
The Snowdonia Way
The Wales Coast Path
The Wye Valley Walk
Walking in Carmarthenshire
Walking in Pembrokeshire
Walking in the Forest of Dean
Walking in the Wye Valley
Walking on Gower
Walking on the Brecon Beacons
Walking the Shropshire Way

INTERNATIONAL CHALLENGES,
COLLECTIONS AND ACTIVITIES

Canyoning in the Alps
Europe's High Points

ALPS CROSS-BORDER ROUTES

100 Hut Walks in the Alps
Alpine Ski Mountaineering
  Vol 1 – Western Alps
  Vol 2 – Central and Eastern Alps
Chamonix to Zermatt
The Karnischer Hohenweg
The Tour of the Bernina
Tour of Monte Rosa
Tour of the Matterhorn
Trail Running – Chamonix and the
  Mont Blanc region
Trekking in the Alps
Trekking in the Silvretta and
  Ratikon Alps
Trekking Munich to Venice
Trekking the Tour of Mont Blanc
Walking in the Alps

AFRICA

Walking in the Drakensberg
KilimanjaroThe High Atlas
Walks and Scrambles in the
  Moroccan Anti-Atlas

PYRENEES AND FRANCE/SPAIN
CROSS-BORDER ROUTES

Shorter Treks in the Pyrenees
The GR10 Trail
The GR11 Trail
The Pyrenean Haute Route
The Pyrenees
Walks and Climbs in the Pyrenees

AUSTRIA

Innsbruck Mountain Adventures

The Adlerweg
Trekking in Austria's Hohe Tauern
Trekking in the Stubai Alps
Trekking in the Zillertal Alps
Walking in Austria
Walking in the Salzkammergut:
  the Austrian Lake District

EASTERN EUROPE

The Danube Cycleway Vol 2
The Elbe Cycle Route
The High Tatras
The Mountains of Romania
Walking in Bulgaria's National
  Parks
Walking in Hungary

FRANCE, BELGIUM
AND LUXEMBOURG

Chamonix Mountain Adventures
Cycle Touring in France
Cycling London to Paris
Cycling the Canal de la Garonne
Cycling the Canal du Midi
Mont Blanc Walks
Mountain Adventures in
  the Maurienne
Short Treks on Corsica
The GR20 Corsica
The GR5 Trail
The GR5 Trail – Benelux
  and Lorraine
The GR5 Trail – Vosges and Jura
The Grand Traverse of the
  Massif Central
The Loire Cycle Route
The Moselle Cycle Route
The River Rhone Cycle Route
The Way of St James – Le Puy to
  the Pyrenees
Tour of the Queyras
Trekking in the Vanoise
Trekking the Cathar Way
Trekking the Robert Louis
  Stevenson Trail
Vanoise Ski Touring
Via Ferratas of the French Alps
Walking in Provence – East
Walking in Provence – West
Walking in the Ardennes
Walking in the Auvergne
Walking in the Brianconnais
Walking in the Dordogne
Walking in the Haute Savoie:
  North
Walking in the Haute Savoie:
  South
Walking on Corsica

GERMANY

Hiking and Cycling in the
  Black Forest
The Danube Cycleway Vol 1

For full information on all our
guides, books and eBooks,
visit our website:
www.cicerone.co.uk

CICERONE

Trust Cicerone to guide your next adventure,
wherever it may be around the world...

Discover guides for hiking, mountain walking, backpacking,
trekking, trail running, cycling and mountain biking, ski touring,
climbing and scrambling in Britain, Europe and worldwide.

Connect with Cicerone online and find inspiration.

- buy books and ebooks
- articles, advice and trip reports
- podcasts and live events
- GPX files and updates
- regular newsletter

cicerone.co.uk